What Shape Tomorrow?
Important Issues Facing the
Local Church in the 21st Century

STRAIGHT STREET
PUBLICATIONS
P.O. Box 608 • Kaneohe, Hawaii 96744

WHAT SHAPE TOMORROW?

Straight Street Publications
P.O. Box 608
Kaneohe, Hawaii 96744

Ralph Moore and Daniel Brown
WHAT SHAPE TOMORROW?

ISBN O-9628127-3-0
Printed in the United States of America

10 9 8 7 6 5 4 3 2

On a "street called Straight," scales fell from the eyes of Saul of Tarsus. It was there that he began to see the way that led to establishing the Church in new territories. It is our goal to stir your thought and increase your vision for expanding the Church into all nations.

Oops!

:T

ii 96744

Beginning on page 68
from "Miscellaneous,"
the remaining paragraphs
were inadvertently inserted.

TABLE OF CONTENTS

The Power of Weakness
  Rick Allen 9
Paint Fence. Wax Car.
  Michael Bagby 21
Balance is a Myth
  Daniel A. Brown 33
The Steroid Church
  Wayne Cordeiro 43
Submission: Event or Lifestyle?
  Gary Craig 57
A Pastor's Place in the Life of People
  David M. Edwards 71
Confessions of a Pharisee
  Tom Gardner 79
The Task of Foursquare Missions as it Relates
to the Church Both Locally and Corporately
  Frank Greer 91
Leadership: Defining Greatness
  John Honold 103
Reclaiming Ministry to the Wounded
  Mark Hsi 113
Understanding Why They Died
  Gary Matsdorf 123
Jesus the Disciple Maker
  Jeff McKay 131
Perspectives From a New Kid on the Foursquare Block
  David Moore 139
Equipping Ministry In Search of a Model
  Ralph Moore 153
Are We a Business or Are We the Church?
  Ron Pinkston 165
Self-Differentiation: Finding Your True Voice
  Sam Rockwell 175
Looking Beyond the Obvious
  David Sather 185
Attitudes for Revitalizing a Local Church
  John A. Tolle 193

What Shape Tomorrow?
Important Issues Facing the Local Church
in the 21st Century

An American prophet once declared, "the times they are a changin..." Two and a half decades of gut-wrenching roller coaster history proved him right.

We've come all the way through the antiwar protests of Vietnam to the heroics of Forrest Gump. The Jimmy Carter inflation gave way to the Ronald Reagan prosperity. The George Bush victory in the Persian Gulf paved the way for the vacillations of the Clinton presidency. Families must sport two jobs to survive. The murder rate is at a recent high. Schools no longer allow religious influence, but open their doors daily to gang recruitment. Churches bar their windows and give up on evening meetings in fear of neighborhood violence. The United States is a decidedly different place than it was before the social revolution of the seventies.

The recent cry for morale values and the shift to the right in the U. S. Congress bode for more change. A major revival is the obvious solution and people seem ready for it. Nevertheless, social chaos and a call for morality also gave rise to Adolph Hitler and company just two generations ago. Change is tricky stuff and demands our attention. In ancient days, "the people of Issachar knew the times and what Israel ought to do." In a cry for their insight, we invited a handful of promising young leaders to Honolulu to discuss our changing times. The event was the second Issachar Symposium. We asked that each participant write a paper addressing the question, "What is the most critical issue facing the church in the next ten years?" No experts were involved. Each read his paper aloud, and every view was as important the others. The discussions grew intense but love oiled the process as iron sharpened iron. The exercise stimulated thought and built confidence. Many came intimidated by fear of writing. They left ready to put words into magazines. Each man grew a new circle of friends in the process.

This book is a compilation of those papers. It represents growing leaders and their view of the next ten years. You will discover that they see the early 21st Century pregnant with opportunity in the midst of continuing upheaval.

We trust the book will do two things for the reader. The obvious wish is to produce hope and a challenge for a greater ministry. The second trick up our sleeve is a secret desire to see you duplicate the symposium in your part of the world. Pastoral gatherings *can* be participatory if we find a supporting format. Paul's words in I Corinthians 14:26 would suggest that the Holy Spirit still has much left unsaid and waiting for a hearing.

Your friends and fellow servants,

Daniel Brown
Ralph Moore

THE POWER OF WEAKNESS
A Treatise On The Advantage Of Dysfunction And Its Relationship To The Gospel Of Jesus Christ

Rick Allen

We do not hear often enough the truth that in our weakness God's strength is perfected.[1] Christians often believe God's power is perfected in divine deliverance from circumstances, and secular society worships victimization as an escape from responsibility. Few on either side of the spiritual line believe weakness can be of benefit to either God or man. This paper seeks to reveal the power of neediness; to encourage Christians to embrace, not escape, states of physical, emotional or spiritual need that demand God's grace. I believe many Christians have lost sight of the fact that our *need* for God always provides an opportunity to *glorify* God. In this paper I do not limit the definition of indigence to physical lack; rather, I define it as "anything we believe hinders or distracts us from being fulfilled." The world may view this problem as *dysfunction*, yet God sees it as *a constant opportunity for His love and grace to be made known to man.* It seems *need* is a dirty word to some in the faith. The premise of some theologies within the Church is "overcoming need by performance": if we can think, believe, confess or act our way out of a state of need we are deemed spiritually successful. Some believe this "success" grants us increased favor with God. We are encouraged to have faith in our faith, or faith in our works, rather than faith in the sovereignty of God. Need, therefore, often becomes a compromise of success rather than a possible means of glorifying God. This is a faulty theology, since we must believe our favor before the Lord is established only and completely by the blood of Jesus Christ and His righteousness and remains static from that point of redemption. Our performance is irrelevant to gaining God's approval - our righteousness is filthy rags and our sins are remembered no more. Although a maturing spirituality is unquestionably a tangible result of being known and loved by Him, identifiable performance is a fruit, not a root, of a relationship with God.

In the secular arena the fear of lack and the worship of success produce the cultural gods of tolerance, subjective truth and civil liberties. When we fear being responsible for our own actions or beliefs we establish a philosophy of life that secures protection from blame and consequences. For fear of being assessed, we exalt tolerance. For fear of being held accountable, we dismiss absolute truth. For fear of conforming to a higher standard, we raise the banner of civil liberties. The ungodly exercise their devotion to these deities at the altar of social cause: an opportunity to prove the inherent goodness of mankind through good works and politicized compassion, and to find excuses for our human nature by defining dysfunction as an unfortunate result of victimization rather than a product of sinful nature. Yet in all its publicity and accolades the social agenda of meeting needs *around* us remains shackled to the insatiable desire to meet the perceived or real needs *within* us.

Dysfunction is our culture's convenient whipping-post; a cross upon which we crucify our responsibilities in life. It is increasingly cliche to discredit so much of what is labeled "dysfunction" as merely escape from responsibility; and to highlight that pop-psychology has found another way to define sin without admitting its source or awful ramifications seems redundant. The more difficult task is to recognize that the kingdom of God offers an answer to dysfunctionality not merely through the availing of oneself to God's power to overcome it but by understanding fully that <u>in</u> our weakness God's strength is perfected; meaning, the first step in bridging the chasm between man and God is always *human need for God's love and grace.*

The reason some Christians find it difficult to embrace weakness as a perfection of God's strength is simple: many believers remain devoted to the same "power theologies" the world is enamored by, and are convinced that faith means power, power means earthly success and earthly success means increased favor with God. How often is a member of the Body of Christ asked to speak at a conference based on his or her *weakness*? Divine grace as an answer to human need has to some become unacceptable. Anything short of tangible deliverance from, or definable causes of, our need is often discarded as an absence of faith or lack of revelation. We live in a culture (both church and secular) where more honor is given to those who are strong, to those who display few if any signs of weakness. God (Whom, it seems, loves to level the playing field of life), takes this and nearly reverses it–*exalting* that which seems foolish to the world and its ways.[2]

Jesus defined the relationship between human neediness and God's favor differently than what is expressed by some in the Church today. Jesus declared *blessed* are the poor in spirit, those who mourn, the meek, the persecuted, etc.[3] While we try to escape being needy Jesus declares neediness a blessed state. Jesus defined the power of indigence with His life:

> "For you know the grace of our Lord Jesus Christ, that though he was rich, yet for your sakes he became poor, so that you through his poverty might become rich."[4]

James reminds us:

> "Listen, my dear brothers: has not God chosen those who are poor in the eyes of the world to be rich in faith and to inherit the kingdom he promised those who love him?"[5]

The writer of Hebrews tells us the *weaknesses* of such notables as Gideon, Barak, Samson, Jephthah, David, Samuel and the prophets were turned to strength; causing them to become "powerful in battle, routing foreign armies."[6] Paul reminds us Christ was "crucified in *weakness*, yet he lives by God's power."[7] Additionally Jesus declares in the parable of the Great Banquet that it is the "poor, the crippled, the blind and the lame" whom God desires for His kingdom.[8] So why do so many Christians reject the possibility that their dysfunction may perfect God's strength? The answer may reside in our natural tendency to work our way to heaven; accepting God's free gift of salvation through Jesus Christ will always be our biggest step of faith.

The farther we travel from the fundamental truth that all imperfection in man is based in sin, and that man cannot earn his way to heaven, the more likely we are to increasingly (and more creatively) justify our failures and subsequently dismiss the need for, or belief in, God and His plan of redemption. Many Christians are enticed to hide their need for God from the glaring eye of modern Pharisees (those who turn the New Testament into law), or ascribe blame for their weakness to that which has no defense of itself (an inheritance, a past experience or physiological imbalance). Instead of wasting our time and energy on searching for the causes of dysfunction, or in seeking creative definitions of dysfunction, or pursuing signs and wonders to overcome our dysfunction, why not simply *at times* accept our weakness and realize it is an advantage to our relationship with God to need Him?   God is not a respecter of men and continues to love and use both weaker and stronger members, yet God's honoring of weaker vessels should challenge our definition of acceptance in God's kingdom. Despite how cliche it has become the truth remains: many of us would reject the original twelve disciples as potential pastors or church leaders simply because they were rough around the edges, unlearned or cultural misfits (dysfunctional). How many of us would label Paul harsh or legalistic and define Peter as a man who "needs more tempering and maturing before being released into ministry"? How many of us today would allow someone like Peter to preach in our church shortly after his public denial of Jesus? (God did and thousands were saved). God truly uses the foolish to confound the wise, and where we see weakness God sees opportunity for glory!

> "And the eye cannot say to the hand, 'I have no need of you'; or again the head to the feet, 'I have no need of you.' On the contrary, it is much truer that the members of the body which seem to be weaker are necessary; and those members of the body, which we deem less honorable, on these bestow more abundant honor, and our unseemly members come to have more abundant seemliness, whereas our seemly members have no need of it. But God has so composed the body, giving more abundant honor to that member which lacked, that there should be no division in the body..."[9]

A further challenge comes when we realize it is God Himself, and not necessarily individual circumstances or choices, that dictate the weakness/strength factor of any given person. Our ministry positions are dictated by Jesus, our gifts are dictated by the Holy Spirit and the final effect of these ministries and gifts are dictated by Father God.[10] The amount of faith we possess is not determined so much by pursuit as by divine providence.[11] We seem not to have much to do with the enforcement of God's kingdom except for obedience to Him. The agency of free-will does have its influence, yet we are constrained as lumps of clay to not question the intent or goals of the Potter:

> "...who are you, O man, who answers back to God? The thing molded will not say to the molder, 'Why did you make me like this,' will it? Or does not the potter have a right over the clay, to make from the same lump one vessel for honorable use, and another for common use?"[12]

Many cry out to God, "Why did you make me this way?" or even, "Why did you make *them* that way?" Accepting God's *ability* to make vessels of honor and dishonor is relatively easy; accepting God's *desire* to do the same is difficult, for it presupposes that weakness is valid in God's eyes, and this is an affront to our success-oriented culture. Could it be possible some among us are weak by divine design?

Unity in the Body of Christ may well come when we stop trying to fix everyone, (including ourselves), and allow for a seemingly disparate lot of people to function as God has called and equipped them; and acknowledge that God's acceptance of us is based completely and solely upon the blood of Jesus Christ:

"Accept the fact that your need for growth does not affect your acceptance [by God]."[13]

As true as that statement is, I sometimes have a hard time accepting it. For most of my life the definition of love, formed by whatever processes and subsequent beliefs, was performance oriented: "...a commitment to compel another person to realize and succeed at fulfilling their calling in life." This definition sprouted from the fertile soil of classic dysfunctionality (child of alcoholics, broken family, etc.) I am now learning a <u>new</u> definition of love: "...a commitment to help another person fulfill their calling, and serving them *whether or not they fulfill their calling*." This definition leaves an uncomfortable amount of room for error and weakness, yet certainly finds basis in the Gospel.[14]

Encountering substandard performance in someone's life often compels me to not only diagnose the symptoms but search for the root cause of this "aberration." I've found the compulsion to identify root causes of behavior may circumvent the ultimate purposes of God, and the identification of root cause itself may be inconsequential to someone's healing or performance. Take for example the account of the blind man healed by Jesus in John 9:1-3. Jesus' disciples are curious as to the cause of the man's blindness, asking, "...Rabbi, who sinned, this man or his parents, that he should be born blind?" Jesus answers, "It was neither that this man sinned, nor his parents; but it was in order that the works of God might be displayed in him." It mattered not what the root cause of the man's blindness was, nor was his indigent state a cause for pity. *The man's affliction set the stage for God to be glorified.* It wasn't that long ago where my response to someone's "blindness" was like that of the disciples in John 9...to spend more energy on ascribing blame and developing systems of improvement than making room for God's sovereignty.

It may also be true that in our attempt to find the cause of our dysfunction we may also be unearthing things God has buried as a part of our healing and on-going need for Him. I often wonder, when approached by someone who through intensive counseling has "remembered" a hurtful incident in their life, if there is a reason that incident was buried in the first place. Is it possible God knows we would be unable to handle the trauma and therefore protects us from it? This is not to suggest we completely turn a deaf ear to causation counseling, since root causes may indeed hold the key to freedom. Still, we should allow God the freedom to define the type and time of our healing...buried past and all.

The basis for this paper is far from academic. Dare I say, risking offending the more religious among us, the foundation for this work is *experiential*. Among the many manifestations of "dysfunctionality" in my life one event in particular exposed the wonders of being needy. It began before I was a Christian, at the age of 16, installing a stereo system in my Ford Galaxie 500. After nearly breaking my hand a few times attempting to remove my dashboard, and going through more than few wires and connectors, something happened that scared me to death. At the time I didn't know what was happening, I only knew I was in trouble. A sudden surge of fear coursed through my body, my heart began to pound as though it were coming out of my chest. I broke into a cold sweat and could not control the shaking that caused the tools to drop from my hands. I thought I was going to die. Racing into the empty house in a panic I looked for something, anything, to calm me down. Nothing worked. I finally laid down on our living room floor, curled up into a ball, and rode the storm out.

I never told anyone about the incident, fearing I would be labeled crazy or forced to discover I had an incurable disease. It wasn't until years later and long after committing my life to Christ, following another such incident, I realized I needed help. My condition was finally diagnosed as "panic attacks."

Although it is not my intent to explain a "panic attack" in either emotional or medical terms I will sufficiently say they are scary, uncontrollable and very disabling. My first reaction to the diagnosis was a sense of failure, for I was raised believing weakness was unacceptable. My panic attacks increased in frequency and intensity over time, and like anyone else I examined the possible causes of these attacks; from diet to spiritual bondages. I also sought counsel, and while many had opinions, few had answers. There were those who screamed and panted over me in an attempt to cast out demons, and others who offered the abyss of on-going psychological counseling. As diverse as the responses to my plight were those I received counsel from had one belief in common: *these panic attacks cannot be from God!*

One night before going to bed I sensed a panic attack looming over the horizon of my evening. I prepared myself prayerfully, and entered the storm. Thoughts of failure besieged my mind: "I'm a Christian! I'm a pastor! I have authority in Christ! What is wrong with me?" Suddenly the voice of the Holy Spirit intervened:

"You'll rarely be this close to Me, not in this lifetime. Be still and know that I am God."

As the word penetrated my soul the Lord unveiled the awesomeness of His love; for I was at such a depth of need I was lovingly cornered into an intimacy with God I'd never experienced! My time with God during that panic attack was rich with peace and hope. I became a child in the arms of a Father. The experience was so deeply rewarding that from that moment forward I never again feared panic attacks, even looking forward to them as a means of relying on God completely. This response may seem peculiar to some who still equate weakness with a loss of God's favor. I understand this perspective, having been steeped in performance philosophies and theologies all of my life. I'm still a workaholic and remain inclined to demand much of myself and others around me, yet I have found a place of refuge in my weakness that clearly brings freedom to me and to those around me.

Since accepting my dysfunctionality as a means of being close to God the panic attacks have ceased. Still I recognize the lasting effects of my ordeal: although I experienced a deliverance from panic attacks I still possess enough weakness to insure God's strength in my life. I am a weaker vessel who has received more honor from God...the honor of being in need of Him and thereby giving Him the chance to prove Himself faithful.

As a father I understand the power of need; for when my sons *need* me I am more blessed and fulfilled than when they are simply *with* me or doing things *for* me. As long as I am glorifying God by being needy why should I seek to escape this dependency? I feel sorry for some who are not classically "dysfunctional"; those who love God but rarely seek Him because their needs are met through the tangible rather than the intangible. What a joy to know without God I am doomed! Of course the accuser of the brethren believes my weakness is a defeat, just as he believed Calvary was Jesus' defeat. Yet Satan is victorious only to the extent we allow him to be and when we remain of "good cheer" in the midst of our trials and tribulations we defeat him. Why? Satan knows better than we do our acceptance in God is based solely on the blood of Christ. If we allow even our weaknesses to glorify God we have truly made Satan impotent; for if he cannot accuse us in our *weakness*, our most vulnerable state, he loses a significant weapon in his arsenal. It is important to note the words of Jesus in John 16:33:

> "I have told you these things, so that in me you may have peace. In this world you will have trouble. But take heart! I have overcome the world."

Jesus spoke these words in response to His disciples' inquiry about Jesus leaving "in a little while" to be with the Father. Jesus tells them, "...you will weep and mourn while the world rejoices. You will grieve, but your grief will be turned to joy." And, "...now is your time of grief, but I will see you again and you will rejoice, and no one will take away your joy."[15] Our hope is not in the victory of *battles* but in the promised winning of the *war*. Whether we win or lose on any given day should not dictate the degree of our hope, but the assurance of Christ's victory over sin, death and hell should be the residence of our hope. Jesus left room for our weakness by compelling us to look at His final victory and not our erratic performances in this life.

Just as the Apostle Paul declared, may I, too, boast in my weaknesses that God may be glorified! Wouldn't it be revolutionary for a host of believers to accept God's grace rather than breach it, and *boast* in their dysfunctionality–not as a point of sloth, lack of faith or pride but as a profound point of victory? Job proclaimed:

> "Though He slay me, I will hope in Him. Nevertheless I will argue my ways before Him."[16]

Job declares two important truths: we can trust God in any circumstance, and God is never intimidated by our humanity. Paul begged the Lord three times for freedom from his "dysfunctionality." Where Paul sought freedom in the physical, God supplied freedom in the spiritual. Where I sought freedom from panic attacks I found intimacy with God *in the midst of them.* It was my faith in God's ability to meet my need *during* my panic attacks that caused a deliverance from them...not my ability to overcome them myself. My weakness also supports a level of empathy for others and keeps me from the arrogance of "What's wrong with these people...why don't they just get up and move on?!" Paul writes:

> "...to keep me from exalting myself, there was given to me a thorn in the flesh, a messenger of Satan to buffet me–to keep me from exalting myself! ...Therefore I am well content with weaknesses, with insults, with distresses, with persecutions, with difficulties, for Christ's sake; for when I am weak, then I am strong."[17]

And...

> "For I determined to know nothing among you except Jesus Christ, and Him crucified."[18]

What a wonder it would be if we held true to God's Word and concerned ourselves only with the paradox of Christ's crucifixion, and our daily crucifixion, and presented our weakness as a trophy of God's grace and not a failure to attain earthly success.

How then do we encourage others to remain flexible and see dysfunctionality as a possible means to victory and not defeat? As a pastor I must ask myself this question: is my sincere attempt to "free" someone from their dysfunctionality, whether by preaching, teaching, counseling or prayer, possibly thwarting God's purposes? Not that I always remain content with my ailments or the afflictions of others; just content with God's answer to those needs. Nor would I encourage someone to manufacture a dysfunction in order to get close to God. Our very existence as humans defines dysfunction; there is no need to search further.

God may indeed relieve someone's distress as a part of His plan. Yet how do we accept the real and tangible *grace* of God in the midst of our neediness? Regarding dysfunctionality, my goal now is to employ the following:

1. Admit weakness (Romans 7:7-25). I used to avoid this, yet have found it to be one of the most liberating "ministries" I engage in. I make it a point to sensitively expose my failures, confess my sins and be held accountable not by a selected few but by *all* those I serve. This accountability is not entered into in a manner of asceticism nor without appropriate parameters of righteous diplomacy. Like Paul, I "...boast all the more gladly about my weaknesses, so that Christ's power may rest on me..." and "...for Christ's sake, I delight in weaknesses, in insults, in hardships, in persecutions, in difficulties. For when I am weak, then I am strong."[19]

2. Accept grace (Romans 8:1). I try to get as excited about grace as I would a miraculous healing since both are divinely implemented and intended for my benefit. Sharing my experiences in life and highlighting the truths of God's Word, I encourage others to look again at their weaknesses and find where God's strength is perfected; to ask the question, "Is this condition or circumstance God's way of getting my attention, humbling me or proving just how much I need Him?" I accept grace (receiving forgiveness I don't deserve) and mercy (being released from judgment I do deserve) as reminders of my need for God and as motivators of righteousness.

3. Assent to God's desires for our growth and healing (II Corinthians 12:8; I Peter 2:1-3; II Peter 1:5-9). It would be foolish to lie down and accept every weakness that befalls us without first contending for healing or deliverance. Just as Paul pleaded three times for deliverance from his thorn in the flesh I petition God until I'm instructed by Him to cease. It is also a mistake to accept the measure of our spirituality today as the limit of God's purpose for us. Fruitfulness (a measurable quality of increasing spirituality) is important to God. Jesus tells us that Father God removes every branch in Him that does not bear fruit yet prunes even the fruitful branch that it may bear more fruit.[20] Pursuit of spiritual fruitfulness is therefore appropriate, yet we must be willing to accept God's parameters and purposes of our pursuit. Where Paul sought deliverance *from* ailment, God supplied humility *through* ailment. I believe God always desires wholeness for us...it is God's definition of that wholeness with which we must be content.

4. Avail ourselves to trials and tribulations (John 16:33). Jesus *promised* believers they would face trials and tribulations in this life. Since challenges in this life are unavoidable I encourage people to *welcome* the storms of life, *despite their origin*, as a means of driving us to the shelter of God's wings and forcing us to examine the foundation of our life in Christ. As shown in the story of the blind man in John 9:1-3, the origin of weakness or calamity is often irrelevant; yet the state of indigence itself may be an opportunity for God to be glorified. If I never experienced infirmity I would never know Jesus as Healer. If I never lacked I would never know Jesus as Provider. If I never hurt I would never know Jesus as Comforter. The trials of life also help to rid us of unnecessary baggage, forcing us to prioritize our beliefs and resources; and they reinforce our relationship with Jesus, compelling us to see Him as our only hope.[21] I encourage people to become "storm resilient" rather than "storm avoiding" by walking through storms with them, exposing my own storms in life, and highlighting the promises of God that assure victory for God's people despite the circumstance.

5. Avoid the worship of earthly success (I Corinthians 3:19). Success defined *qualitatively* is more essential than success defined *quantitatively*; still many in the Body of Christ remain affected by cultural definitions of wholeness and health. Measuring Jesus and His disciples by today's standards of success we can easily declare them failures. After nearly four years of intense ministry attended by incredible signs and wonders with thousands filling temples and mountain tops in fellowship with Jesus, His closest disciples were nowhere to be found as Jesus hung on the cross. Only about 120 disciples were left to gather in Jerusalem in anticipation of the promise of the Holy Spirit. If this happened to a church or ministry today we would call it a failure or describe it as "in decline." When we start acknowledging divinely commissioned weakness as strength and resist measuring the activities of the Church by earthly standards we will see more of God's glory and less of man's glory. An equally accurate measure of fruitfulness in our churches today may well be the number of parishioners *leaving* because we preach an uncompromised gospel and remain devoted to making disciples and not merely converts.

As much as God desires wholeness for His people He also desires our dependance upon Him. While we contend for healing and deliverance, we should be content with God's answer to our prayers. Our weaknesses are <u>always</u> an opportunity to glorify God, and dependance upon Him must return to a place of honor and not disgrace. We must stop equating earthly success with Godly favor, and instead define "success" as God did for Joshua: *possessing Godly discernment*.[22] With discernment we see the power of weakness and the foolishness of fearing indigence. For the cause of unity, aligning ourselves with God's purposes we should give greater honor to those who lack honor, and treat the less honorable with special honor.[23] In doing so God's power is perfected.

NOTES

1.   II Corinthians 12:9
2.   I Corinthians 1:18, 25; 3:19
3.   Matthew 5:1-12
4.   II Corinthians 8:9
5.   James 2:5
6.   Hebrews 11:32-34
7.   II Corinthians 13:4
8.   Luke 14:21
9.   I Corinthians 12:21-25a
10. I Corinthians 12:4-6
11. Romans 12:3
12. Romans 9:20-21
13. McDowell, J. and Bellis, D., Evidence For Joy. Waco, Texas., Word Books. 1984. Pg. 138.
14. Ephesians 2:8-9
15. John 16:20 and 22 respectively.
16. Job 13:15
17. II Corinthians 2:7b and 10
18. I Corinthians 2:2
19. II Corinthians 12:9b-10
20. John 15:1-2
21. Romans 8:28-39
22. Joshua 1:8
23. I Corinthians 12:9

PAINT FENCE. WAX CAR.

Michael Bagby

And one of them, a lawyer, asked Him a question, testing Him "Teacher, which is the great commandment in the Law?"

And He said to him, "'YOU SHALL LOVE THE LORD YOUR GOD WITH ALL YOUR HEART, AND WITH ALL YOUR SOUL, AND WITH ALL YOUR MIND.'"

"This is the great and foremost commandment."

"The second is like it, 'YOU SHALL LOVE YOUR NEIGHBOR AS YOURSELF.'"

"On these two commandments depend the whole Law and the Prophets."

Matthew 22:35-40

When we ask ourselves the question "What mandates do we have for life here on Planet Earth," we come down to two basic commandments: "Love God", and "Love your Neighbor."

Loving God is the top priority of any of person here on the planet. Loving God means to place Him Number One in your life, to follow Him, and be His disciple.

Being a disciple in the spiritual environment here is not an easy task. There are many hurdles to overcome; starting from our own free will, to the natural order of this world, to the spiritual opposition of Satan and his cadres.

Yet from the moment we make a decision to follow Jesus, and be His disciple, He begins a work in us–a work to change our character into one more like His.

"Therefore if any man is in Christ, he is a new creature; the old things passed away; behold, new things have come."

2 Cor 5:17

We often try to orient ourselves in the right direction and pursue spiritual growth through formal programs and informal events, but ultimately He is the one who does the work.

As Paul said in Phil.2:13: "For it is God who is at work in you, both to will and to work for His good pleasure"

How is it that God works to cause this spiritual growth to occur?

There are at least two obvious methods, and a third that is a bit obscure.

First, we grow spiritually by reading, studying and mediating on God's Word. Psalm 1 says: "How blessed is the man who does not walk in the counsel of the wicked...but his delight is in the law of the Lord; And in His law he meditates day and night. And he will be like a tree firmly planted by streams of water, which yields its fruit in season, And its leaf does not wither, And in whatever he does, he prospers."

This is the easy road to spiritual growth. Some people are gifted with the ability to absorb God's truth, incorporate it into their lives, and allow their actions to be conformed accordingly. Most of us aren't and that's where God's second method comes in.

Psalm 66 says: "For Thou hast tried us, O God; thou has refined us as silver is refined; Thou didst bring us into the net; Thou didst lay an oppressive burden upon our loins, Thou didst make men ride over our heads; We went through fire and through water, Yet Thou didst bring us out into a place of abundance." (Ps.66:10-12)

The second method that God uses to mold our spiritual character is through trials and tribulations. This is often an effective method of changing our character, but it is not pleasant. James says to "Consider it all joy, my brethren, when you encounter various trials..." (James 1:2) This is definitely not my preferred method.

The third method that God uses to mold our character is one which at first seems a bit ambiguous, because it comes from the "second greatest commandment" given by our Lord. He told us to "Love our neighbor."

Loving your neighbor means getting to know him, spending time with him, helping him. Ultimately "Loving your neighbor" means to be involved in serving him. The New Testament is full of commandments to do something for "One Another." We are commanded by Paul numerous times in the New Testament to specifically involve ourselves in a service to one another.

Now this commandment has obvious value when it comes to the needs in the body of Christ and the work of the Kingdom here on Planet

Earth, but there is a deeper purpose here...a purpose that goes far beyond the obvious intent.

Remember the movie "Karate Kid"? Here was a guy who wanted to learn karate. He showed up for lessons eager to learn some karate moves. But his teacher told him on the first day to go "Paint Fence." The boy was surprised, and reluctantly spent all day with a brush moving it up and down over the boards.

The next day the boy arrived tired but still eager to learn some karate moves. His teacher told him to go "Wax Car." Disheartened but obedient, he went with rags and spent the day moving the cloths in circular motions over not one but a whole fleet of classic cars owned by his teacher....."Wax On...Wax Off."

The next day the kid arrived for lessons, and the teacher assigned another mundane chore. The boy protested. "I want to learn about Karate" he screamed in frustration. It was then that his teacher suddenly moved forward and with his hand tried to hit the boy. The boy reacted quickly and naturally, and with a circular sweeping motion, prevented his teacher's hand from striking him. Then the teacher moved in with another punch- this one a little higher. The boy again moved naturally and quickly. With a smooth up motion of his hand he easily deflected the blow.

Suddenly the light went on. The boy realized that the previous hours of "painting fence" and "waxing car" had trained his hands to move in a natural karate style motion. These mundane chores were the means by which he learned to defend himself.

In God's third method of molding our character, we are told many times in the Bible to "love one another" and "serve one another." Yet in the book of Ephesians, Paul tells us of a deeper purpose of these commands:

> **"He gave some (gifts) as apostles, some as prophets, some as evangelists, and some as pastors and teachers, for the equipping of the saints for the work of service, to the building up of the body of Christ; until we all attain to the unity of the faith, and of the knowledge of the Son of God, to a mature man, to the measure of the stature which belongs to the fullness of Christ."**
>
> Eph. 4:11-13

Men were given spiritual gifts. Why?

To prepare other men and women for works of service.

Why are work of service important?

So that the body of Christ will be built up. Why?

So that we may all grow in our spiritual character and become mature.

According to Paul, God has gifted men to train the members of the body of Christ in works of service (ministry) which will build up the body of Christ. These works of service will lead to greater spiritual maturity on the part of the individual members and the body as a whole.

Involvement in ministry is a means by which spiritual growth occurs.

When I was a younger Christian, I was deeply affected when I read Ephesians 2:10. This verse talks about how we were "created in Christ for good works." Like many other Christians I latched on to this concept as my "raison d'etre"- the thing that now gave my life purpose. I began to focus on these works, not realizing there was a deeper purpose for these works.

Let's face it, any problems that the church is now tackling through the various ministries in progress could be solved with a snap of God's fingers- if He wanted to. But for some reason, He doesn't. Many times, He chooses to work through us. He wants us involved in the process of actively loving and helping others. To me, **that alone is a clue that there is a deeper purpose here.**

The attitude that the average Christian has toward the "works of the Church" directly affects his spiritual well being. Some are so focused on the work, that they ignore things like developing relationships, family priorities, and an attentive relationship with the Lord. "Works" become their ticket into the Heavenly realm. They forget the basic "salvation by grace message" and religion and legalism dominates.

On the other hand, those that hold fast to the "saved by grace" theology are not very active in the various programs and ministries of the church. They become fat lazy Christians who want nothing more than to be fed on Sunday morning. They never get involved in any of the programs of the church (except perhaps on the receiving end).

Both these groups suffer from a false understanding of the purpose of being involved in the ministry of the Church.

For those who do participate in the various ministries of the church, many can look back and see that when they involve themselves in the lives of others, something happens inside. It is a spiritual dynamic. You can't help but be affected when you pray with someone with a terminal disease. Holding a dying malnourished baby in your arms for the first time definitely touches something deep inside. Working with a single parent or a person with sexually transmitted deadly disease causes something to change in your spirit. Seeing children respond to teaching on the Word of God or a family rebuild their relationships on Godly principles is exciting. Both bring a growth in your faith in the power of the Word.

It is a Spiritual Dynamic: when we involve ourselves in the lives of other's by loving them and serving them, growth in our spiritual character occurs. That's one of the reasons why Paul commanded the people in the early church to be involved in ministering to one another.

Now realizing the basic mandates of our Lord, and some of His methods for making disciples, what are some of the ways that we can proceed effectively?

One of the most effective means of growing spiritually is through involvement in foreign missions.

There is a move today among many local churches in the United States, Canada, Europe, and Australia to get directly involved in world evangelism, church planting, and building up established churches in third world countries through discipleship, medical relief, and spiritually oriented development programs. Until recently, this work in the past has been done through denominational agencies, or "missionary societies," with the local churches' part having been mostly financial support for these institutions.

One of Jesus' last commands to His disciples (us) was an all inclusive order to "make disciples" wherever we happened to be. We realize that missionary work happens (or at least it should be happening) in every place where there is an established part of the body of Christ, be it Honduras or Honolulu. For the sake of this discussion, let us define "missions" and "missionary work" to be the spreading of the Gospel in a foreign culture outside of your native country.

Some in the body of Christ are called to devote all, or a substantial part their lives to serving within another culture outside of their native country, and are involved in long term projects and outreaches in this foreign culture. Short term missionary work is usually a project or outreach undertaken in support of a long term work. This usually involves local volunteer church body members applying their special skills or spiritual gifts within a time frame of two weeks to a year.

This last decade especially has seen an increase of participation of the local church in missionary work through teams or individuals sent out from the church directly to missionary agencies and projects in the third world. Enthusiasm for this sort of direct participation in missionary work is growing, as local body leaders and members begin to realize the benefits of their direct involvement.

Why should a local church be directly involved in missions?

What are some of the things that happen because of their participation?

Why should a pastor look for opportunities to get himself and members of his congregation directly involved in foreign mission work?

1) First of all, a greater awareness will develop in the local church of the worldwide mission and responsibility of the body of Christ (including the local church) to take the Gospel into all corners of the world, and make disciples in all the nations. The natural inclination of a local church is to focus within their walls and communities. The "Great Commission" directs our attention to other peoples and places **as well as** our own communities.

2) Greater utilization of individual spiritual gifts and skills will result by participation of local body members in foreign ministry. Many "first world" Christians have skills that are needed by our brothers and sisters in Christ in the third world.

In earlier times this would have been difficult due to the time required to "qualify" for foreign service, or family and job requirements at home. Relatively cheap and fast air travel has made short term missionary work feasible. The needs of basic skills in the developing world are tremendous.

3) A more realistic approach to life (and ministry) here on Planet Earth will be taken by individuals within the local church who are participating in a foreign mission project. Local body problems often seem overwhelming until one is exposed to the daily challenges of third world life. Less than 7 % of the body of Christ has a standard of living matching ours (United States-Europe-Canada). Changes in perspective and priorities often occur among "first world" Christians after working directly with the third world church, and a more realistic focus on the real issues results. Real issues for 93 % of the Body of Christ don't include concern over thickness of carpet in the sanctuary, or the size or style of the pastor's desk, or the color of the drapes. They do include tomorrow's meal, and the health of the family.

4) A more direct targeting of local body resources to projects and outreaches in the developing world happens when there is direct involvement by a local church in a foreign mission project.

The command to be good stewards of what God has given us has been often compromised in the past by "impersonal" financial giving to multi-layered organizations. **The object is to have the greatest percentage possible of what is given reach the purposes for why it was given.** This percentage increases dramatically through direct participation of a local church with established projects and ministries in the third world.

5) Tremendous support and encouragement is given to the long term missionary workers by the direct involvement of supporting churches. This personal contact reduces and eliminates many of the adverse effects of living for extended periods in a foreign culture. Visits by to the mission project for the sole purpose of encouraging the foreign missionary have tremendous value, which cannot be overstated.

6) Some local church members are today feeling the call to dedicate substantial portions of their lives to the work of the Kingdom within a foreign culture. The natural hesitancy to leave their "comfort zone" can be reduced, and this call can be confirmed through a short term missionary project.

And now the most important reason for a local church member to get directly involved in a foreign mission project:

7) We have found that many internal spiritual changes occur when a first world Christian participates in ministry in the third world. The spiritual dynamic of serving and loving others is accelerated by the change in physical cultural surroundings. God seems to move in more dramatic ways. Maybe that's **because in a foreign setting your dependence on Him dramatically increases** since you have stepped outside your "comfort zone" and away from an environment that you have a large degree of control. You depend on Him for such simple things like transportation, health, eating, and sleeping.

In our experience with mission teams over the last ten years, we have seen profound and dramatic spiritual growth occur over a relatively short period in many individuals. Most of these so impacted were "primed" for spiritual changes to occur, and the process of "Paint Fence and Wax Car" in a foreign environment accelerated a process that was already beginning. Many members of these teams have later commented to us that this period was one of "the most spiritual times" of their lives.

For us, of all the reasons for a local church to directly involved in world missions, this one of personal spiritual growth is probably the most important. The direct link between the local church and the foreign mission agency and project is a "bird killer". With one "stone", many things are accomplished, including what we have found to be the most effective way of allowing or promoting the most important process in our personal lives to occur- that of ourselves being a disciple of Jesus and being molded more into His character.

The Challenge

Living within a foreign culture away from your native country presents very substantial psychological, sociological, and spiritual challenges. To try to work within that foreign environment is even more difficult. To work effectively on a long term basis can only be done with language skills, an advanced level of cultural understanding, certain "professional" skills applicable to the actual project, and a willingness on the part of the "missionary" to endure certain physical and psychological hardships.

The often stereotype view of missionaries as those who were unable to "make it" in the States, and for that reason came to the mission field is unrealistic. To follow the call of the work of the Kingdom in a foreign culture requires a measure of faith not often found in many local body members. To handle successfully the multi-level challenges of life within that culture, requires a particular aptitude and ability. To have success in the work of the mission, long and short term, requires a high level of determination and discipline.

It also requires a definite program of orientation and preparation.

For the local body church member feeling the call to long term missionary work, or involvement in a short term project, the opportunities for "orientation" and "preparation" for work on the "mission field" have been very limited. This orientation/preparation has usually been available through a denominational program, or through a formal education program at a Christian college, both of which involve long periods of time, and which is geared toward the "long term" player.

Orientation/preparation programs for the short term teams have sometimes been carried out by the sending church at their home location, via shared experiences from previous short term team members, with some cultural orientation. This is valid approach, as long as "shared experiences" from previous teams or individuals constitute a realistic perspective of their experience, which may not necessarily be the case. Our church, Hope Chapel Maui, sends teams each year to the Philippines. Their two week schedule there is packed with events and they are able to present their music/drama/teaching/testimony program to hundreds each day. Their daily level of excitement is high. Many come home thinking that all missionary work is just what they experienced.

Unfortunately that is not the case. Much of our time is spent in routine, slow, and sometimes frustrating work to create and maintain the infrastructure required to allow such intensive activity to occur.

Some short term teams, and prospective long term players arrive on the field with little or no preparation. As a result, their initial cultural adaptation and effectiveness is severely limited.

The challenge as we see it is to effectively use the resources of the Kingdom to further the works of the Kingdom. In the foreign mission field, these "resources" are people, finances, materials, and time.

To send a group of 10 people to a place 4000 miles away from their home to complete a particular mission project or to send a family to a foreign country for years to engage in a long term project are both expensive in terms of all of these resources.

How can we get the most fruit from such efforts? The answer lies in two steps:

1) Being led by the Holy Spirit; and

2) Preparing the missionaries for their mission.

With our logical minds, we can plan how the Lord would use us and where. This we must do. But we must remember that He is the Lord who knows where to best use us and how.

In my own personal experience, since I was a European History major in university, and spoke French, and lived in Europe during my youth, it would seem a natural place to serve.   I was living in Hawaii when I got turned on to the Lord. Our natural focus here is to look west: to Japan, the Philippines, India, China, etc. I had spent a few years in during my time in the Navy living in this part of the world. This region too seem like a natural place to serve.

But when a missionary came to our church in 1984 describing the conditions among Miskito refugees in Honduras and his plan to help, I responded and volunteered to help gather supplies. Soon I volunteered to help deliver these supplies, and left on a typical two week short term missions trip. One thing led to another, and we began a school project which is now in its 8th year. My two week trip turned into ten years. Instead of working in Europe or Asia which seemed like two logical options, I ended up involved in a place that was never on my travel itinerary.

My wife Laura is another example of the leading of the Holy Spirit. She responded to an urge to move from Honolulu to Maui in 1987, where she met me on one of my visits home. She is a social worker and hair stylist who was definitely not the camping type. She married me in 1988, and moved to Auka, a village eight miles form the Honduran-Nicaraguan border. She was one of four American in this village, and our house had no electricity or running water. Laura responded as I never expected, and adapted very well. She learned the language Miskito language quickly, and established many relationships with people in the village. She quickly became an effective cross cultural worker.

It was obvious when we look back that the Holy Spirit was leading both of us to each other and to Central America, contrary to what we would have planned. But we both realize that we were in reality inadequately prepared for the environment and work that the Lord had planned for us. Many of our early years can be categorized as "on the job training." We realize now that there is a better way to prepare the missionary for his work.

We have developed over the years a training and orientation program for short term teams that we conduct during their time (usually 7 to 14 days) with us. This course covers geo-political aspects of the mission, historical background, and cultural adaptation. Not only does this help the short term work accomplish his mission more effectively, it provides a valid framework for them to view and interpret their own experience on the "mission field." This course is also helpful in their influence on their local church body after they return from their mission. **They become world vision Christians with practical experience in world evangelism. Having such members in a congregation cannot help but affect the focus of the local body church.**

For the prospective long term missionary, we are involved in a missions training center at Las Mangas Honduras, which is a working dairy farm located in the mountains behind La Ceiba. Our concept is to teach the practical and language skills required to live in a third world environment, as well as the cultural adaptation required to become effective workers of the Kingdom within the foreign culture. The daily schedule is a combination of classroom training and practical application on the farm, with extended periods of work in isolated villages. We are fortunate to have a staff of "missionaries" with formal education and years of successful practical experience in their own projects.

There are other programs which also successfully train the short and long term missionary. These mentioned here are just the ones that have worked for us.

By relying on the Holy Spirit to lead, and through effective orientation and preparation programs, ministry in a foreign land can be one of the most accelerated ways to grow spiritually. I know that the Miskitos have benefited from our involvement in their lives, but as we look back we realize that perhaps the ones affected most by this work has been us. God has used this project among the Miskito Indians to dramatically change their lives. All of us associated with Project Ezra and Seek The Lamb have been dramatically changed as well. **This project has been our personal vehicle for spiritual character development.**

By us "Painting Fence" and "Waxing Car" here on the Coco River, or wherever the Lord places us, we are forever changed people.

Changing people from "natural" men and women into "Christ-like" members of the Kingdom seems to be God's main order of business here on Earth.

BALANCE IS A MYTH

Daniel A. Brown

You've met Christian leaders, as I have, who exude a sense of unflappable equilibrium — men and women whose steady demeanor and neat coiffure seem to say to everyone around them, "It is well *not only* with my soul, *but* with my schedule, my church and my family *as well*." Or like a pastor friend of mine, they never seem to have any prayer requests that betray even a hint of personal inadequacy or discombobulation.

With my hair and my schedule so often tousled by unexpected gusts (or unremembered appointments), I look longingly at these *together type* leaders and conclude that they could not possibly have the spiritual gift-mix or the congregation I have. Either that or they know something "too wonderful" for guys like me. The daily press — kids late for school, weeds in the garden, three *more* letters in the "to do" pile on my desk, and a father in the church outraged at being reported (by us) to the authorities as a suspected abuser — makes cool composure a distant dream.

That's why I've decided that balance is a myth. At least the kind of balance that can be arrived at once and for all is a myth. I understand balancing (translate that *juggling*) the demands of family time with ministry responsibilities, or filling out doctrine with mercy. A pastor should avoid extremes, laugh *and* cry, filter the latest thing hitting the larger body of Christ through the dual lenses of Scripture and God's assignment to that local assembly. But those sorts of balancing acts are hardly static. Usually they are scrambled reactions to situations that could not be anticipated. Mostly my life is a series of interruptions, crises and challenges that can only be met with cries of, "Oh God, help..." and "Here we goooooo."

Yeah, I know the scriptures about God being the stability of our times ... this hope we have as an anchor to our soul ... His peace passes understanding ...calming the storms ...and rest for my soul. But that's the whole point: balance is not a de facto state; in the stormy ups and downs, when we cannot figure out what's happening around us, we can turn and grab hold of the Lord. Balance isn't supposed to be a badge Christians wear to validate their spirituality — like a birth announcement that on such and such a day baby Balance was born. Balance isn't like immunity to Chicken Pox — once you have it you never need worry about losing it.

The kind of balance I strive for in my life is more like that of a tightrope walker. It is very important to be balanced on the platform. But frankly, that shouldn't be too hard to maintain for someone who has trained to walk a much narrower path. When I step off that little platform with the long pole in my hands, I must shift my weight and my posture *in response to* changing conditions, including my own previous moves.

Balance is a process *through* the many years, not merely a product *of* those years. Experience does make the balancing process a bit easier, just like practice certainly helps the tightrope walker. But just because I have been balanced before doesn't mean I am today! Balance must be maintained actively. So what sorts of things can a ministry leader do to help maintain balance? Here are some thoughts that have helped me (in no particular order):

1. **Every little move makes a difference.** It's not the big things that get you in trouble, but the small sidesteps and slips you are tempted to ignore.

2. **Many things are best balanced over the long haul.** Seasonal changes are usually more appropriate than daily ones, or at least more practical.

3. **God is more interested in me than in my ministry.** Consequently, He will focus more on the development of my *walk with* Him than on my *work for* Him.

4. **I am far more likely to be wrong than right.** It is easier to change when the goal is to *end up being* right rather than to *have been* right.

5. **God wants to change *me* more than the situations or people around me.** He wants to adjust my heart and perspectives, so I conform to His image — not He to mine.

6. **Success is an inner conviction, not an outward show.** Doing what He tells me is more than doing all else.

7. **Stress-free, pressure-free living is not the goal.** Although a balanced lifestyle is healthier for me, the point of my balance is the health it brings others.

8. **Imbalance is a symptom of deeper, underlying issues.** The sins or bondages are probably too systemic to identify on my own.

9. **Ministry and life itself are not about me.** The more I live for the sake of others, the more balanced I will become.

I am sometimes discouraged when yet another need for adjustment shows up in my **priorities** (like increasing my contact with older members of the church instead of newcomers), my **family** (like preparing to be late for our Sat. PM service during soccer season when I coach my son's team), or my **personal growth** (like learning the difference between being right and being righteous). It helps to remember, however, that a false balance bothers God (Prov.11:1); He wants me to have a heart that can sense when the scales have tipped — not just an act that freezes the arms of the scales in an illusion of balance.

DISCERNMENT AND BALANCE

Within the overall sphere of pastoral ministry, nowhere is balance more necessary than in discernment. As with most spiritual activities, discernment does not lend itself to a step by step, follow the numbers approach. If we view balance as a process of weighing one thing against another, we must start the process by acknowledging that there are two kinds of discernment mentioned in the New Testament. Paul records the spiritual gift of "discerning of spirits" to the Corinthians, and Hebrews refers to the practiced ability of learning to "discern between good and evil."

But before we look at discernment itself any closer, let's talk about the need for it in the church. First of all, we know that our foes are not people or circumstances; what hinders and harries us are forces, personalities and powerful entities from the spirit world. Though we may choose to ignore or downplay their role in the way things turn out, they manipulate and frustrate our responses to what is going on in our churches.

Take, for instance, the outspoken man in your congregation who definitely has an attitude about him — the kind of air he has makes you feel that you must let him do whatever he wants. Even though you don't agree with him and despite the fact that you somehow just feel funny about the things he says, you still feel too intimidated (or too mean) to put a stop to the obvious trouble he is causing. Or what about the very spiritual-seeming woman who always leaves you as the pastor feeling like the church would probably be better off if she led it; after all, God is always talking to her (and almost never to you), she prays ten times as much and as well as you, and yet something hits you wrong about her.

Those odd little sensations are probably discernment. God, who charges shepherds to watch over His flock and who tells us to keep a close eye on factious people, is trying to warn us about problems that will develop if we just look the other way. If we don't respond to those promptings, our congregation will end up paying a steep price. Without discernment we will allow such people to influence more and more people by rising to ministry prominence. Intimidation, uneasiness, confusion, fear, agitation — these can be the imprints of evil presences on your radar screen. A pastor who at least sifts those sensations through the filter of Scripture and an assessment of the fruit evidenced in those people's lives will last longer in ministry.

Last week I had a conversation with a pastor who was so traumatized by one particular couple in his church that he quit. They had driven him from his assignment over a three year period ... or had they? As the story goes, the pastor had sensed ripples of rebellion and being second-guessed ever since that couple had started coming to the fellowship five years ago. In the beginning the couple effusively declared their support for the pastor and offered their services to him on the basis of their spiritual compatibility with him. The subtle suggestion was that their spirituality—equal to his—saw fit to go along with his leadership, but the "equal footing" of their spiritual stature with his set the stage for the Absalom undermining that followed years later.

The pastor lacked discernment. So desperate was he to gain people and approval, he didn't recognize the cost being exacted of him by some of those people. When the issue first came to a major point of disagreement — the pastor wanted to have cell groups; the couple refused to agree to cell groups — the pastor avoided the real issue and decided to give the couple time to come around to the idea of cell groups. Cell groups had nothing to do with the real issue, as was proven when the couple put their foot down against hiring a part-time staff person, and when they began to sow discord about very basic administrative procedures instituted by the pastor.

Discernment would have told the pastor that he was dealing with Jezebel, rebellion, pride, a contentious spirit, or a host of other spiritual possibilities. Because he had not tried the couple by challenging them when they were slightly out of step in little matters, he had little recourse left when they were so blatantly off base in big issues. He might still have confronted their sin, but by not discerning the underlying potency of the spiritual root of the problem, the pastor simply quit his post, muttering something to himself about not having to take this from anyone! Had the couple driven him from caring for the flock, or had his own lack of discernment done the job?

Spiritual issues are not always connected with problematic people. Very often the trouble just hangs about like a thick fog, and the church feels discouraged, flat or listless; or, it is plagued with sickness, disorder or financial trouble. Spiritual assault on our church and the people in it (especially us) can manifest in any number of ways: staff problems, local government resistance to building plans, drop in attendance, lethargy and heaviness, etc. A wise pastor knows when to mobilize the church to prayer and intercession against unseen powers that are trying to thwart the purposes of God.

The problem is that not all problematic situations are caused by demonic activity. Sometimes the Lord Himself is arranging things for His own purposes — like Joseph's hard life in Egypt or Paul's seeming inability to take the gospel into certain regions. Our own church has faced unbelievable hassles from local government on two sites we wanted to purchase, and only latter did we realize that God had been saving us from moving too soon and, thereby, missing out on the incredible facility we now lease.

Neither are all the people-related difficulties we face brought about by sinister powers of the air. Many of the people whose sense of direction and mission for our church differed from mine were not gripped by some sinister foe nor were they attempting to overthrow my God-given place in the church. They simply had a distinct calling from the Lord to pursue ministry in a different manner and context than that to which He had called me. Not only was nothing wrong with those dear believers, but my struggles to come to grips with why we weren't seeing eye to eye on things actually helped me clarify my own sense of our church's ministry focus.

Not all trouble is bad, much less demonic.

How is one to know the difference between the deep plans of God (Ps. 92:5), who is up to a greater good than merely answering our immediate and uninformed prayers, and "the wiles of the devil"? What are the things we need to balance in our considerations, and what process can we embark upon that will promise us an accurate assessment of what we face?

Every leader ought to wear a necklace. I don't mean some totem or discernment amulet. I'm referring to the necklace mentioned in Proverbs 3:3, the one with the two precious stones of kindness and truth. For too many years in my Christian life, I neglected the stone of kindness and tried to judge matters solely on the basis of truth. You know, good doctrine, solid scripture and firm instruction. I forgot that you cannot find the truth without first finding the heart of God.

Mercy triumphs over judgement, not because it is stronger, but because God's first impulse is to extend mercy rather than to execute summary judgement. Judgement is easier than mercy. Once I judge people, my job is essentially done; the onus is on them; I am done with them until they see things my way. That can be a trap in discernment — wanting to finish with people rather than to keep with them (and help them be done with their stuff).

It can be easier for me to write off another saint than to simply admit to myself that not every believer in our town is supposed to call me pastor. Rejecting them in the name of discernment is far more satisfying than facing the rejection I feel when people are led away from my church. Likewise, deciding someone is in bondage to rebellion requires much less of me than determining to discover what trauma in their life has made them so fearful of authority. Offering to pray for their deliverance is far less involved than building up a track record of patient compassion with them over time.

Discernment should be a starting point for mercy and restoration. The point of a good medical diagnosis is an appropriate treatment. So it has been helpful for me to check my motives before I settle in on a judgement about what is going on. Do I want a quick fix, an easy assessment to protect me from the more difficult tasks of discipling someone or of believing that God is great and good even when I don't see the answers I have set my hope on?

Spiritual warfare is hard work. Doing battle against unseen foes is no walk in the park. But sometimes a feigned skirmish is easier than actually confronting someone about what they said or did. "Doing battle in the heavenlies" may sometimes be little more than avoiding our leadershipping responsibilities on earth:

> "And the Lord's bond-servant must not be quarrelsome, but be
> kind to all, able to teach, patient when wronged,   with
> gentleness correcting those who are in opposition, if perhaps
> God may grant them repentance leading to the knowledge of
> the truth, and they may come to their senses *and escape* from
> the snare of the devil, having been held captive by him to do
> his will." 2 Tim. 2:24-26

Balance in discernment requires that I take a good long look at myself to be sure that no eagerness for a fight lurks in the corners of my heart. It's just too easy to blame my rotten opinion about a person on a demonic manifestation. That's why I have to keep coming back to kindness — both as the underlying passion of my soul for them, and as the approach I take toward them.

Likewise, before I decide that the reason more people in my church don't volunteer is because they have come under a sinister influence, I better check to be sure that I have taught them adequately on the spiritual benefits of serving. Lack of good teaching will produce the same results as demonic assault in many cases. What some pastors call a spirit of poverty is merely the meager fruit of their poor sowing. A spirit of poverty can exert itself against a congregation that is well-taught on God's patterns for our finances, but that demon will not be able to withstand a determined counter-assault from us.

Patient when wronged. Being a leader and being wronged are almost the same thing! The very ones whom we are called to serve are the ones who will do us wrong. They criticize our decisions (like in the wilderness they grumbled against Moses), they turn their backs on us in favor of another ministry in town, or they leave us out of things that mean alot to us. They whine, they complain and they gossip ... human beings! However, those very human tendencies do not necessarily signal the presence of other types of beings. Just because I have been wronged doesn't mean I am under demonic attack.

And yet, viscous rumors and persistent lies may be the work of lying spirits that are hell-bent on ruining you or your ministry. The key to discerning your foe is personal patience — a willingness to grant people extended mercy rather than getting all worked up the instant you hear that someone said a hurtful comment. By being merciful in your heart toward the person, you will begin to detect the source of the assault. Before you get into a pie fight with the people around you, remember that just because you have been hit by a pie, and just because the person is the only one you see around, doesn't necessarily mean they threw it!

Suppose they did throw it; even suppose they were told to throw it at you. Would the best initial response on your part be to rail against them or what influenced them? A good question to ask is whether or not they have been taught what to do with pies (or observations). The role of an assaulted leader is to instruct not to lash out. With gentleness and humility we should take the opportunity presented to us (by their opposition to us), and train them again. Like a math teacher faced with the wrong answers of a problem-child, we will be tempted to dismiss our responsibility to teach the child in the name of personal impatience.

To the last, Jesus' plea was for their forgiveness.

Jesus knew all along that the devil was the ultimate source of His agonies. Yet He did no battle and offered no threats. He knew that the best way to resist the devil is sometimes to simply suffer (1 Peter 5:9). But that brings up an entirely different subject — what to do with what we discern.

Let's get back to leadership and the role discernment plays in helping us direct the people and the particulars of our churches. Since David was a shepherd raised up after God's own heart, we ought to be able to learn some valuable lessons from the way his discernment functioned.

David's role as king is characterized by two important attributes (Ps. 78:72): integrity of heart and skillfulness of hand. He was both a shepherd who associated with and tended his people, *and* a leader who governed and directed them. Good discernment begins with understanding the difference between these two roles in people's lives. Sometimes we should weep with the weeping, but at other times our role is more to challenge them to move beyond their sorrow. Jesus first identified with us. Only after establishing His willingness to associate Himself with us does He ask for our willingness to receive correction from Him.

Discernment is an act of love for the sake of others—firstly for the person who is in bondage, but if the person does not receive that love, our love for others in the church who might be affected by the bondage bids us, secondly, to take stronger measures for their well-being. After we have established a meaningful relationship with people, it is no longer the loving thing to do to ignore obvious sins or bondages. The wounds of a friend are faithful.

Furthermore, David seems to have three additional roles than that of a king: priest, prophet and shepherd. As king, his duty is to look out for anything that might hinder the orderly pursuit of the national interests. He wants to maintain fair and equitable laws and to make sure that the kingdom is operating smoothly. This gives us valuable clues about our discernment; we should keep our eye on anything that disrupts the basic flow of the church, hindering its administration, its mission or its orderliness. The king wants to know, "Are things being done decently and in order?"

David is a worship leader and a man who leads his people in offering sacrifices to God. He would be very sensitive to any person or force that diminished worship. In our churches we, too, ought to watch for moods, events, people or seasons that dampen our fervor in worship and praise. Since worship is an act of warfare and of celebration, the enemy has particular loathing for it, and he will do whatever he can to remove it from our arsenal in the early stages of an attack on us. That is why I am especially alert to worship as a good barometer to measure enemy activity.

David is also a prophet whose heart burns for God's word. His delight is to meditate on God's words all day long. Without this prophetic bent, David's discernment would be dry and legalistic. In the same way, we must be careful to balance our concern for good governance with a passion for the Word — always checking what is happening around us with the promises and provisions contained in it. Anything not built on the Word of God will perish, no matter how well structured it may be. The prophet always wants to know, "What is God's word to us, and how does this line up with that word?"

David the shepherd cares for the lambs — strengthening the sickly, binding the broken and seeking the lost. He wants to keep the sheep from being scattered and becoming food for the wild beasts. While leading a nation, he doesn't forget to attend individuals. Rather than relying on force and severity to rule over his flock, David seeks their best at his own expense. As shepherds we should use our discernment to spot the broken and the lost, not to write them off. The shepherd wants to know, "How are my sheep doing — are they cared for and nourished; are they secured and strengthened?"

Priest, prophet, shepherd and king — four good reference points with which to balance discernment as church leaders. I find that when I evaluate the situations I encounter with these four perspectives, my conclusions are usually better.

Let me say one last thing about discernment and balance. Never forget about that feeling in your guts that warns you something is wrong. I don't even know what to call it, but the few times I have ignored it because I couldn't reason it out in words, I have ended up regretting it. Maybe a dozen times or so I have had this deep certainty in my guts that has told me to beware — usually about people rather than situations. Though there has been nothing on the surface to explain my "problem" with these people, I've just had a funny feeling, red flags flapping in the wind.

Each time it has turned out that there were huge moral gaps in their lives. The last time was only a few months ago, a leader of a parachurch group who was fired after ten employees finally mustered the courage to risk the spiritually transmitted threats that spewed forth from this man and

his bondage.   Their collective testimony of financial and sexual
transgressions matched exactly with what I had been feeling at a distance.
And my wife had been feeling it even stronger. That is a sure sign ...

Discernment is so subjective that it can easily become no more than
a tool of our own convenience. We can coerce people into doing many
things in the name of discernment. It smacks of hidden understanding, a
thing the mystics used to intimidate novices and outsiders, and it breathes
of superior insights, a claim made by the Gnostics. Discernment parts
company with the reasonable proofs, and in so doing makes itself and us
extremely vulnerable to deception.

But having acknowledged all that, I still think discernment is
essential for a leader. If it is kept balanced in love and in the word, and
if it is used as a tool for the sake of others, then it will greatly aid us in
fulfilling our dual charge of watching over our flock and of presenting
each person complete in Christ.

THE STEROID CHURCH
Tackling the tough questions and side effects of the Mega church

Wayne Cordeiro

PREFACE

As we speed towards the 21st century, it will be of utmost importance to check our ministry compasses. Still reeling from a two decade era of "Church Growth" emphasis, we are now seeing some of the side effects. It has produced a paradigm in the perspectives of young, entrepreneurial leaders. There has developed an unspoken expectation by the leaders who have been platformed at conferences, who have authored books on the subject, and taught in seminaries.

It is my premise that as we enter a new era of church planting and strategic ministry, the time is ripe for us to insure that our course is plotted with points dictated by the issues of God's Word, and not what we have seen come down the highway in recent years.

I have used a metaphor taken from the sports world that parallels my premise. Anabolic steroids hold the promise of chemically prompted accelerated growth. It has swept the world of athletics in every arena of competition. However, the side effects are now surfacing, and the residual effects have often been fatal.

We have been thrown into a current of business oriented, statistically driven church growth strategies. This in itself is not necessarily wrong, however, one of the side effects that often comes as a result of these accelerated growth emphases is a steroidal mentality. This paradigm becomes so systemic that it affects every area of a leader's ministry. I am not suggesting that every large church falls into this category. There are many wonderful examples of large and healthy ministries: The Church on the Way, Beaverton Foursquare, and New Life Foursquare Church in Everett to name just a few. However, big does not always equal healthy.

This paper is written from a diagnostic perspective. It will later be enlarged to include the prescriptive steps. It is my desire that we see as our goal not the "mega church" but to become a "mother church."

INTRODUCTION

We live in an age of new-found heroes. The images we hold in high esteem are no longer the ones wearing white hats. The new giants that inspire our youth are no longer etched out of the granite of character or the marble of integrity. They are now found in the paper pages of *Sports Illustrated*. These modern day heroes, lauded by millions (and paid to the same degree) remind us daily of the value America has placed on not only being entertained, but the premium we place on perfection: in sports, in looks, in body.

We live in an age filled with images of flawless heroes, athletes of perfection, and images of beauty. Thousands of potential hopefuls enter the race each year aspiring to join the elite of these who can jump higher, dribble with more agility, hit the ball harder, pass the football farther, or run faster than anyone else. And the price tag we put on these gladiators lures many to trade it all in for the pot of gold at the end of the buzzer.

Not only in the sports arena but in every arena of life, physical appearance, image, and a perception of self-confidence have attained such an important place in our society that many will do anything to gain its laurels. These men and women are seen as gods or goddesses who live the lifestyles of the rich and famous. They are seen as models and modern day heroes, the apex of the American dream.

This fixation on achievement has bled into every area of life as America tries to copy and clone these images. It characterizes the clothes we wear, the things we buy, the way we act. Beautiful bodies, muscle bound Schwarzeneger's, Bruce Lee's, and Sylvester Stallone's all become the poster dreams in every young person's bedroom.

With this yearning desire to be "created in their images" comes the vast options and temptations to quicker results with less effort. In our image-starved culture comes the promise of immediate perfection, and the golden key to attaining that is STEROIDS. Quick muscle mass, increased stamina, greater strength, a sculptured body texture, and a renewed confidence is just the answer that steroids can promise. Add to that the feeling of invincibility, and you have a lure that few can resist. So irresistible is this elixir that thousands of teenagers are now regular customers.

In the Steroid Trafficking Act of 1990, it is stated that, *"Teenagers take steroids because they 'work.' Steroids are effective in promoting muscle growth. They take it despite the warnings of medical experts about serious side effects of physical and psychological consequences. The use of steroids has been associated with serious physical disorders, fatal liver and kidney failure, hypertension, increased aggression, birth defects, and cardiovascular disorders. The promise that steroids give to young people is shattered when faced with the stark reality of its dangerous and often fatal side effects. Attempting to strengthen the body, the steroid user can destroy the mind."*

STEROIDS AND CHURCH GROWTH PRINCIPLES

In the last two decades, the Christianity has been involved in a "Church Growth" era where it has explored different avenues to produce accelerated congregational growth. Seminars, conferences, and church consultants promised larger crowds, greater results, more sculptured ministries, and a new feeling of confidence. One advertisement in a Religious Broadcasting magazine read: "Win 10% of Your City To Jesus Christ In One Day!" Books began to abound on church growth. Many began to make their living as "Church Growth Consultants," and the new buzz words like *"Mega-church,"* and *"Church Growth Barriers"* separated the men from the boys.

However like the steroidal approach to body building, there is now beginning to surface the many side effects such as hypertension, heart disease, and birth defects. The last two decades have seen the producing of the mega-churches we have today, but the price has been steep.

Recently at a pastors seminar, two pastors and their wives of some of America's largest and fastest growing churches shared deep hurts and wounds, some yet to be healed, that they experienced while building these mega-churches. A pastor's wife from the city in which I pastor has just gone through an emotional breakdown. At a Portland, Oregon conference, another mega-church pastor woefully admitted to a hurt and struggling marriage which has been to him a "wound that just doesn't seem to heal." His wife, feeling alone at home most of the time, went back to school during those solo years, and she now teaches in a nearby college. His son, not wanting to have anything to do with his father's lifestyle, rebelled. Have we forgotten our second generation? We can mention numerous other pastors having heart attacks, broken marriages, and those struggling with rebellious children, and the list would go on.

Our obsession on size and muscle mass has affected even our perception of the Church. We are living in an era where the "Mega-church" is platformed as the epitome of spiritual blessing and ultimate success. The mega-church pastor is asked to share his secrets of accelerated church growth, and the steroids are purchased in neatly packaged programs, injected or swallowed whole.

Some of the more potent strains of steroids are imported from home and abroad. They come in from Korea, Los Angeles, or other sources of mega-growth. But, please don't misunderstand me. These *sources* really don't manufacture steroids. We simply import them, and somewhere in the cloning process (or attempted cloning process), a steroid is manufactured. In our fixation for "big and beautiful bodies," we get caught up in the euphoric desire and drive to be like our counterpart. However, God never intended us to be a copy of Korea or Timbuktu. We must learn from them, gather ideas and lessons from them, but never to the point where we jettison our own assignment and identity in exchange for the hopes of a bigger, more beautiful body in thirty days.

THE MUSCLE CHURCH VS. THE MIGHTY CHURCH

In Acts chapter two, we find the beginnings of the Church as God intended it to be. Men an women devoted to prayer, in one mind, trusting in the Holy Spirit's leading and anointing. The simple Gospel is preached. No gimmicks, no technique, no pretense, no feasibility studies, no grand marketing schemes. Three thousand is added in one day. Fairly impressive church growth.

The church in the Book of Acts had hardly any of the resources that occasion our shelves today. No tapes, seminars, computers, polls, or research groups. They didn't even possess the Bible as we have it today. Yet we find mentioned with great frequency miracles, healings, salvation, baptisms, people being discipled, and people moving in leadership. **It was a Mighty Church!**

Today's Church, compared to all other years of Christiandom, is the wealthiest of all time. We have more resources, seminars, tapes, music, facilities, seminaries, and notable teachers than any era. In any given week, somewhere in the United States you can find a seminar about some aspect of Christianity being taught. Information and secrets abound that promises accelerated church growth. Books from how to "Cook for Christ" to "101 Ways to Grow Your Church" are yours for the asking. We are rich! But are we mighty? There's a big difference between being a muscle-bound church and a *mighty church*. Being big isn't necessarily being <u>healthy.</u> Are we getting caught up in a steroid generation of church growth? How much of the octane that fuels church growth is really *us*, and how much is genuinely the Holy Spirit? Is it growing by ministry or by methods ... by character or by "chemicals?"

As we approach the 21st century, we need to take stock of who we are and what we may be fast becoming. There's still time to turn the dials and recalibrate our course before the side effects do lasting damage. We cannot afford to be one-generational thinkers. We owe it to our King, and we owe it to those who will come after us. As it says in one of our contemporary songs, *"May those who come behind us find us faithful."* That will be the greatest legacy we can leave them.

Let's look at four side effects of the *"Steroid Church."*

Side Effect One: The Ever Rising Bar

I am convinced that some of the Kingdom's greatest heroes are the unsung heroes. The ones that no one will ever recognize. They will never appear on the covers of *Christianity Today*. They will never be a headline speaker at a mega-church conference, and they may never receive accolades from publishers. We have left them far behind. A new hero in Christian circles has emerged, lauded in conferences and magazines. Their names are equated with success and spirituality. Their lives are profiled as those with whom God is *"well pleased."*

It was in the decade of the fifties that the pastor with the longest tenure was considered successful. This was the one who could outlast his critics and stay at the helm despite the storms. Then came the decade of the sixties. Here the bar would rise another notch, and now the successful pastor was not the one with the longest tenure, but the one with the largest congregation. Notch three brought the decade of the seventies where it wasn't just the ones with the largest church.. The ones who were spotlighted as successful "body builders" were the ones who built the largest churches in the *shortest amount of time!*

Then just when hopeful pastors were breaking their backs (and their marriages) to attain that dignified honor, the bar was raised another notch. Now in the eighties, it wasn't just the ones who built the largest churches in the shortest amount of time, but now it was "all the above" *PLUS* pioneering the most churches in the process. This killed off most of the stragglers, and only the strongest survived.

Then just when we were building a new strain of budding mega-pastors, the bar was raised again. The decade of the nineties ushered in the need for a new breed of "body builders." Now it was those who not only built the largest churches in the shortest amount of time while pioneering the most amount of churches in the process. Now it included those who could spin another plate by writing books in their spare time (with their favorite subject being: *"How Every Neurotic Pastor Can Maintain a Healthy Family and a Joyful Marriage While Building Another Mega Church.)*

When will it all stop (or when will it kill us? ... Whichever comes first.)

One of the subtle side effects of the steroid mentality is that *"It's never enough."* It doesn't matter what the count is on Sunday morning. There should have been a few more! Twenty were saved? We could have twenty five next time. A church in Asia prays two hours every morning? Let's pray three. The church down the street pays $20,000 a month for mortgage payments? We'll pay $25,000! Church growth principles became a drug of "Growth Fixation." And like any drug, gradually more and more was being required to produce the same level of euphoria, so the drive for *"Bigger-Means-Better"* continued to pick up steam amid cheers, accolades, ulcers, and lonely wives.

We've set ourselves up for a self-induced depression, self-inflicted hypertension, and "joy" becomes an elusive dream we preach about but never really experience. We begin to justify exaggerations about our size while at the same time knowing who we really are and being depressed about it. We experience something called "megorexia." This malady is something a steroid user has that causes him to be unconsciously but constantly comparing his body to others and always coming up with a sense of inferiority. He is addicted to mirrors and always sees himself as a scaled down version of who he really is. This distorted body image is narcissistic in nature, and he finds himself in a vicious cycle of posing and assessing, posing and assessing.

Side Effect Two: Heart Failure

In the book "Death in the Locker Room," Dr. Bob Goldman enumerated the many body builders who have died of cardiovascular disease, myocardial infarction, and other cases of heart failure. This is just one of the many fatal side effects of steroid use. In the athlete's utter fixation on building a big and beautiful body, he *ruins his heart*.

Steroid usage in the church growth era has also caused heart disease. As I travel, I have found many of these "body building" pastors who love crowds *but don't love people*. They enjoy the adrenaline, the pristine feeling of controlling a crowd, but they have lost a deep compassion for the individual in that crowd. There comes an impersonal shallowness that rises in tandem with the body count.

In Mark 5:25-34, we find the story of Jesus healing a woman in the crowd who had an issue of blood. Although a large crowd pressed in on Him, He was cognizant of an <u>individual</u> who approached Him with faith. Jesus saw not only the crowds, but he loved individuals.

> *"When He asked, "Who touched Me?" his disciples answered, "You see the multitude pressing in on You, and You say, "Who touched Me?" And Jesus looked around to <u>see the woman</u> who had done this..."*

It is under this "steroid spell" that Christian leaders have a "heart failure" for the individual person. Every new person is evaluated simply in light of what he or she can contribute towards the fulfillment of the leader's goals. They are not viewed any longer as individuals who have needs, hurts, and dreams. People begin to be viewed in terms of what they can contribute rather than by what they mean to Jesus. These individuals, who instead of being treasured *independently* of what they can offer or how many others they can bring to the church, are seen as *"giving units."* Under the influence of steroids, people are *used* instead of developed.

With this comes a subtle change from having a "serve-others" heart to a *"serve-me"* heart. In fact it is so subtle, many will operate for years without ever recognizing the fact that they have this debilitating problem. It is virtually undetectable, and even when it is, it can be easily justified or spiritualized. It is cloaked in evangelistic fervor and spiritual virtue. We are quick to encourage the congregation to the "highways and the byways to impel the lost" to next week's service or to a special meeting. Invite your friends! Pass out fliers! Advertise and call!

On the surface, it seems righteous and so fulfilling of the Great Commission, but in reality, the octane that fuels our energies shows that "Me" is on the increase, and "He" is on the decrease. Behind the virtuous ringing of "Bringing in the Sheaves" is the subliminal motive scrolling across the screen like a stock market ticker-tape ... *"Bring them in, one and all! The more the merrier! Call the people in and fill the room because what I really need are greater and greater crowds to validate me and to validate my ministry!"*

A former steroid user who now works with adolescents says, "Steroids are being used mostly by men and women and young kids just for their egos. It blows my mind! They are using it for one reason only, for their egos. The peer pressure is enormous, and if you are not gifted or a rock singer, you'd better be big!" [1]

One of the side effects is the user begins to perceive the whole world as revolving around his body, his looks, and his opinions. In today's church growth era, our zeal for greater "body counts" is often sourced in *"me."* In fact someone once said you could pull the Holy Spirit out of half of the churches in America, and they would keep right on operating as if nothing happened. Tragic but true. We must realize that a true heart for ministry cannot return to our pulpits until we recognize the side effects of the steroid church and come home to Jesus Christ. What matters is not the size of the "body count." What really counts is size of the heart. We cannot be moved by numbers. Like Jesus, we must be <u>moved by compassion</u>. Then, and only then, will we again see the supernatural ingathering of souls that so frequently occasions the Book of Acts.

Some time ago, a member of the congregation in which I have the privilege of serving in, came to me after reading the Book of Acts, and commented, "Man, I'd give anything to live in Bible times like these!" he said, waving his Bible in the air. "All those miracles, healings, and thousands getting saved. What a rush it would be to have lived in Bible times!"

I remember responding to him that the "Bible times" he spoke about was not a chronological period of time or an era relegated to history. "Bible times" are simply times in which man chooses to live according to the inerrancy of the Word of God, holding it in high esteem, and forging his life accordingly. These "Bible times" can be today, for *"Jesus Christ is the same, yesterday, today, and forever" (Heb. 13:8).* His Presence and power is not bracketed to a period in biblical history. It is available to all whose hearts are set on Him (2 Chron. 16:9.) And because Jesus Christ is the **SAME** yesterday, today and forever, what He said, He is STILL SAYING, and what He did, He is STILL DOING! The 3000 that were added was HIS doing, not the disciple's efforts, and what He did, He will be more than happy to do again and again.

Side Effect Three: Psychological Disturbances

> Another of the many side effects of body builders is the increased risk of psychological disturbances, increased aggression, frequent periods of depression, a tendency to one-track mindedness, and an increasing desire and drive to excel.[2]

Categorized under the heading of "hypertension," we can see many similarities and symptoms in the "steroid" approach to church growth of the eighties and nineties. Archibald Hart, Dean of Psychology at Fuller Theological Seminary, has said recently that over 60% of pastors suffer from some form of adrenaline addiction and hypertension. Their unbalanced living has accelerated their "dying" and our infrequent periods of renewal are not adequate to slow the downward spiral of our disintegrating marriages, families, and even our personal souls.[3]

This "unbalanced living" has greatly influenced our perception of the whole church growth concept, ministry philosophy, and even theology itself. Are we manufacturing unhealthy pastors? The side effects are beginning to take its toll on our families and marriages.

Recently in speaking with a prominent pastor, our discussion turned to his recent consideration to step out of full time ministry. The reason he gave was that he felt that it was not possible to be in a dynamic ministry while maintaining a balanced, healthy family. The two concepts in his mind could not rationally coexist. If he were to be a faithful father and husband, the only avenue was to leave the full time ministry of this large church and get an eight-to-five job somewhere.

This scenario speaks reams of the tension that many pastors live under, and should this continue, we as leaders will begin to produce a dysfunctional Bride, and that will produce unhealthy, genetically impaired offspring.

Side Effect Four: Birth Defects

The Canadian Medical Association Journal, in an October 1978 article, after lengthy research and case studies, concluded that "The major drawback (of steroid usage) is the fear of genetic damage.[4] Citing Dr. Bob Goldman's research, he found that "Anabolic steroids have been noted to affect genetic integrity, and the risk of birth defects rise dramatically with the use of steroids."[5]

There are two considerations we must grapple with when thinking about "birth defects." Healthy pastors tend to have healthy churches, and dysfunctional ones produce the same. Two Scripture references tip us to a principle we will do well to consider:

1. *"A good man out of the good treasure of his heart brings forth what is good, and the evil man out of the evil treasure of his heart brings forth what is evil"* *(Matt. 12:35).*

2. *"Like people, like priest"* *(Hosea 4:9)*

"You Are What You Eat"

First of all, we find here that each pastor will have the inclination and predisposition to reproduce congregations who tend to view life from the same vantage point as his. This isn't necessarily something bad. Even Paul said, *"..we offered ourselves as a model for you, that you might follow our example" (2 Thess. 3:9).* Nevertheless, we as pastors and "models" must realize the responsibility we have. We must constantly recalibrate back to the heart and motives of Jesus Christ. The focus gets to remain on people: winning them to Christ, recognizing their value and gifts, then developing them so they too will have the heart of Jesus to reach others. If we are not careful, church growth will come to refer more to such things as location, marketing, architecture, programs, and head counts than to maturity of the body of Christ.[6] In a recent poll researchers asked pastors how they believed Christ would rate their church if He were to return today. **Less than 1%** believed that He would rate them as effective, and a whopping 53% felt Christ would find the church as having little positive impact on souls and society![7]

What an astonishing confession from the leaders who shape tomorrow's Bride! But that really shouldn't surprise us. We see the side effects of that lack of direction and purpose all around us. A recent article in the Oregonian read, *"Religion Up, Morality Down."* It summarized its findings that although the crowds attending churches are up, the lifestyles of these attendees were found to be hardly any different from those who claimed no relationship with Christ at all. Watch even an hour of Christian television. In a "me" society, we have refashioned the gospel to fit our culture and generation. God becomes a "Celestial Genie" who we call upon to help us get where _we_ want to go. God becomes Someone who helps us fulfill _our_ purposes and plans rather than His. We pray very little any more about His will being done, and a whole lot more about our will. We no longer come together to worship God. We come together to have a *"worship experience."* The spiritual value of a service is no longer based on the accurate preaching of the Word of God with an appropriate and God pleasing response. Instead it is evaluated based on *"how it made me feel,"* and *"what it did for me."*

Wanting to "look good," pastors in the contemporary church tend to cater to the taste buds of the post war generation. A recent poll was taken asking people what they were looking for in a church. Their number one was: "fellowship" and "good sermons" to "youth program" and a church that "makes me feel good." I ask myself the question, "What happens when the Word of God does surgery and you don't happen to *"feel good?"* What if the message happens to puncture your "happy bubble?" If we are not careful, we will lean in the direction of culture, dilute the Message of Life, and even possibly lean so far as to fall off the edge and into the abyss that runs the way of extinction.

> *"I don't go to religion to make me happy. I always knew a bottle of Port (whiskey) would do that. If you want a religion to make you feel really comfortable, I certainly don't recommend Christianity." (C.S. Lewis)*

According to a *USA Today* survey, of the 56% of Americans that attend church, 45% do it because *"it's good for you;"* 26% cited *"peace of mind and well being."* None of them mentioned anything about worshipping Jesus Christ or about being conformed to His image. This survey, one sociologist observed, was simply a reflection of the "culture of narcissism."

The body building push of the nineties, in order to make themselves more attractive to church shoppers, will unconsciously cause us to fall in line behind one of today's leading humanists, Ted Turner. In a speech given by Ravi Zacharias, he quotes the avowed humanist as saying, "We have no right to tell people what they should or shouldn't do in today's culture. Christianity has had two-thousand years to try and fix the world, and they've failed. The absolutes of the Bible are obsolete. They have been left found wanting. We (man) must take the lead now."

Churches across the country are falling prey to the "McChurch" identity and thereby losing their true identity altogether. An example of this is Denver's Full Gospel Chapel, which was once a conservative mile marker in our directionless society, has changed its name to the Happy Church.

"It draws people," states the pastor.

We can fall prey to this subtle philosophy. In wanting to draw a greater crowd of sympathetic hearers, we will tend to airbrush a word here and soften a command there. It won't just re-texture our pulpits. It will actually begin to change the very character of the Gospel.

No, I am not against the attempts that are made to relate to a media culture with a seven minute attention span. We must be creative and innovative in presenting the Gospel, but behind all the music, programs, lights, skits, and fanfare must stand a solidly orthodox message of deep, undefiled theology. This alone will stand the test of time and will reproduce well.

"A Chip Of the Ol' Block"

A further consideration of churches built by the steroid paradigm is that these possess a greater risk of passing on a "genetic impairment" to their second generation of daughter churches. We realize that one of the "givens" in our accelerated church growth era is the fact that mandatory seminary education is no longer a priority, nor is it even feasible. Time, distance, and family restraints simply exclude all but the young and the restless or those who are married without children. Seminary prohibits those who in their later years have been called to the ministry. Bible College and seminary sometimes presupposes that the majority of ministry calls from the Lord will occur before one's twentieth birthday or at least prior to repeating the vows of "I do." (We forget that Moses began his ministry at 40 years of age, and the apostle Paul was probably thirty-something when he "saw the light.")

Nevertheless, it has become apparent to growing churches that in order to reproduce and pioneer new works, they need to develop individualized and tailored training programs. These localized preparation schools are usually taught by the pastor or a church staff member. Then after sufficient months of observation, assigned reading and the successful handling of certain ministry projects, a full fledged "reverend" graduates to tackle the multifaceted responsibilities of pastoral care, counseling, preaching, finances, vision casting, conflict resolution, and a host of other responisbilities. This poses in itself a problem we will need to face in the years ahead. Unless these men and women are self starters and voracious readers, we will end up with obsolete leaders in one generation ... people who hold "positions" but who are left with archaic, outdated tools.

But what is a greater cause for concern is the "genetically impaired baton" we pass to those who come after us. The defects we carry will have a multiplier affect on our "children." Are we reproducing for the sake of simply procreating *our* vision, or are our children the natural result of a healthy relationship with the "Bride?" Is our heart genuinely concerned with reaching the lost or reaching our goals? Will we pass the baton of our neurotic push to grow bigger and more beautiful bodies along with the myriad of side effects that have proved so debilitating in its consequences? If it has managed to do it heinous work in our generation, can we expect it to do any less in the next?

A DIAGNOSTIC CHECK

> "If a church disguises its identity and preaches a message intended to keep everyone in a state of perpetual bliss, then its growth is man-made. "Growth for growth's sake can be spiritually deadening," says Richard Neuhaus. "Institutional growth is the last refuge of ministries that are spiritually sterile."[8]

As we approach the 21st century, it is of extreme importance for us to take a fresh and honest look at where we have come from, where we are now, but most importantly, where we are headed. Sometimes we get rowing so hard and so fast that we don't take the time to check to see if we're even headed in the right direction. Any experienced navigator knows that he must check his compass not just once when he leaves the port, but often.

It is my premise that we renew the very spirit of our minds in the area of Biblical church growth. The spotlight must be taken off of "mega-church" and onto the **"Mother church."** We are in dire need of a new model before the side effects debilitate us any more. The consequences of the steroid church are not simply encumbering. They are fatal. It is this *"mother church"* perspective that will help us correct the side effects and become healthy as we enter the 21st century. The very term "mega church" has incorrect connotations attached to it. As leaders, we have the responsibility to message a more accurate perspective that results in health and natural (rather "supernatural") growth.

> *"The lamp of the body is the eye; if therefore your eye is clear, your whole body will be full of light. But if your eye is bad, your whole body will be full of darkness. If therefore the light that is in you is darkness, how great is that darkness!" (Matt. 6:22,23 NASB)*

When Jesus speaks about the lamp being our "eye," He is not suggesting our eye ball. He is speaking about our attitude towards something, our perspective. If our perception of the Church and church growth is unclear, it will indeed affect the "Body," and the dark side effects are beginning to show. It is time to recognize the need to change, and do it. We must return to the example and heart of Scripture, set aside our personal agendas and ego needs, and accurately serve *"God's purposes in our generation"* (Acts 13:36.)

It was in Mark 7 that Jesus chastises the Pharisees for neatly setting aside the commandments and directives of God for the "traditions of men." He said that they were actually *"invalidating the Word of God by their tradition which you have handed down"* (Mk. 7:13 NASB).

Are we handing down our own "traditions?" Whose baton will we be passing on? What legacy will we be leaving for those who will come behind us?

> *"According to the grace of God given to me, as a wise master builder, I laid the foundation, and another is building upon it. But let each man be careful how he builds upon it" (1 Cor. 3:10).*

NOTES

1. "Anabolic Steroids: An Ethnographic Approach," Paul Goldstein, pg.79, A Government Pub., 1992.

2. "The Macho Medicine," William Taylor, MD, McFarland & Co. Inc. Publishers, 1991.

3. Taken from a speech given at LaJolla, Calif., October 1994, "Balancing the Pastor's Personal Life."

4. Canadian Medical Association Journal, October Issue, 1978.

5. "Death in the Locker Room," Dr. Bob Goldman, Patricia Bush, Ph.D., The Body Press, Tucson, Arizona, 1984.

6. "The Body, Being Light in the Darkness," Chuck Colson, Word Publishing, 1992.

7. "George Barna study cited in the EP News Service, Feb. 7, 1991.

8. "The Body, Being Light in the Darkness," Chuck Colson, Word Publishing, 1992.

SUBMISSION: EVENT OR LIFESTYLE?

Gary Craig

Introduction

As the men of today's church realign themselves with God's word and His purposes for their lives, submission becomes a forefront issue. Submission is not an intuitive response to leadership, even Godly leadership. Men tend to think of submission primarily as a female issue, an element of a wife's role in marriage. However, everyone is called to submit and it is the responsibility of pastors as leaders to set an example and to instruct today's church, especially men, in the principles of submission.

Some topics are more difficult to approach than others. Tithing quickly comes to mind, both because it addresses a deeply personal area, finances, and because it seems that the pastor stands to gain personally from the response of the people. For the same reasons, submission is not a popular sermon topic. Yet, it is the responsibility of the pastor to lead and disciple others in the full Christian walk.

Teaching others to submit provides an opportunity for the Holy Spirit to convict us of the quality of submission in our own lives and to challenge us to lead others into submission from other than a self-serving perspective. To be effective in teaching others to submit, we must begin with such a self-examiniation.

A number of questions help us in this self-examination. Are the people who are submitted to me getting a good return on their investment? Are they feeling safe? Am I honoring their trust? Are they experiencing significance? Are they learning how to lead others by watching how I lead them? Are they learning how to submit to me by watching how I submit to my leaders? Are they learning how to teach others how to submit to them by watching me teach them how to submit to me?

There are many aspects to submission. Our discussion will touch on the voluntary choice of submission and the safety of submission, but the focus will be on the tendency to view submission as an event rather than a lifestyle and how to combat that tendency. Men tend to view life as a series of goals and if submission is simply viewed as an event to be practiced only when required, then its power will be lost.

Although the major emphasis is on the inner dynamics and personal struggles of the person choosing to submit, two equally important tenents of submission warrant brief consideration. 1) authority exists to serve those in submission. 2) authority encourages the voice of loyal opposition of those it serves.

Godly authority is loving authority. It offers itself to promote others and suffers on their behalf. Authority that puts the interests of others ahead of its own is an environment where submission thrives.

Wise authority recognizes that submission is not agreement. Authority needs to be surrounded by those who will speak the hard truth, who will say, "The emperor has no clothes." Submission is not about blind and silent compliance, but includes faithfully declaring when authority is missing something. This paper deals with releasing the voice of authority and establishing a foundation from which submission may speak.

The Choice of Submission

To submit is to voluntarily place oneself under the authority of another. Submission is the choice of the one doing the submitting. True, there are serious consequences to refusing to submit according to biblical principles, but it is not the perogative of the leader to require submission. Rather, the leader simply offers his/her leadership as a place for others to live. It is up to others to choose whether or not to live there.

Another way of saying this, in grammatical terms, is that submission is a reflexive verb, which means it is something one does to oneself. What is often forgotten, both by the leader and the follower, is that submission is for the benefit of the one doing the submitting. It is a common misunderstanding to consider submission as a statement of relative value, i.e. that the one submitting is acknowledging a greater worth or value in the leader. Yet the issue is not one of superiority, rather of freedom, freedom to be and live as Jesus intends.

There are many scriptures about submission. People may choose to submit to God. Employees may choose to submit to their employers. Church members may choose to submit to church leaders. Wives may choose to submit to their husbands. Believers may choose to submit to one another. Citizens may choose to submit to their government. In all these cases, submission is clearly the scriptural response, but it remains the choice of the individual doing the submitting.

The choice to submit is not an easy one even when submission is understood as proper alignment in the Kingdom of God intended to bless and release the person doing the submitting. Submission is often perceived as for the leader's benefit, so there are many depictions of submission as an act of shame or humiliation, despair or resignation, weakness or failure.

In fact, submission is an act of dignity, hope and strength. There are many different relationships of submission, and though the particulars differ, the principles remain the same. Submission is an act of will and an agonizing one as demonstrated by Jesus in the Garden of Gethsemane.

The Safety of Submission

To be under another's authority is to enjoy a spiritual covering. To submit is to acknowledge our need for leadership, to express our desire to learn, to release the insight, discernment and wisdom of our leaders into our lives. True, we are responsible for our own decisions and there are numerous examples of abusive authority to be found. Yet the existence of error in no way diminishes the power of truth. Let us not too quickly dismiss the danger of being unsubmitted in the face of Jonestown or Waco. The point is that all too often we apply these drastic examples to less than cataclysmic, even routine situations.

There are many blessings that flow from submission. Chief among these is the safety of living according to God's order. Submission is the essence of relationship in the Kingdom of God and Jesus is the primary example. We are safe only when we are submitted, even if that submission leads to death, as it did with Jesus.

Each of us yearns for safety, but we can't provide safety for ourselves. We seek God and ask Him to protect us and keep us safe, but if we ignore His instruction to submit, then we have removed ourselves from the primary source of safety He has placed in His body. It is so easy to call out to God in desperation, all the while ignoring the simple truth that He works through people. When we imagine that we can be submitted to God without being submitted to people, we deceive ourselves.

Submission: A Variety of Perspectives

Recently I have had encounters with three different men which help to illustrate different pespectives on submission: a church visitor who lives a life of open refusal tosubmit, a church attender who casually avoids submission and a church leader who is unknowingly involved in engaged resistance to submission.

A gentleman visited one of our weekend services and began to distribute some printed material on forgiveness. The handout was scriptural, kind and well-written. I invited him to fellowship with us so that we could get to know each other, but to please refrain from passing out material to people that he didn't know. He insisted that God had told him to do it and repeatedly quoted Acts 5:29, insisting that he must obey God rather than men. When I assured him that in this case he didn't have to choose, he left, unhappily quoting his favorite scripture.

One of the most argumentative responses to authority is the misuse of Acts 5:29, "We ought to obey God rather than men." Rather than pursue a lengthy discourse on civil disobedience or conscientious objection, let me just make the simple point that within the Body of Christ, there is rarely the requirement to choose.

Another gentleman had been attending our weekend services regularly for a few weeks. As we chatted, we began to talk about the role of cell groups in our church and the need we all have to live in accountability and submission. He openly acknowledged that he wasn't really submitted anywhere and didn't particularly see the need, but he wasn't caustic. Over the weeks, he has been getting more involved in our church family, and although he definitely has leadership qualities, it will be interesting to see how he responds when he is faced with a situation where submission becomes an issue.

A third gentleman is actively involved on the leadership team of another congregation. He asked me some questions, particularly about the allocation of church finances between property resources and personnel resources, including his own compensation. He believes that his pastor and church board, of which he is not a part, are making unwise and unjust decisions. Having made a laborious effort to convince his pastor of a different perspective, he was asking for evaluation of his use of God's word.

He did invite me to speak frankly and although his questions dealt with the biblical accuracy of his opinions, I responded that I believed the issue was one of submission and that he needed to seriously evaluate his attitude toward authority in his life and make some tough decisions. I assured him that I have no authority or perspective on whether or not he is being treated fairly, but the much more significant issue has to do with his relationship with his pastor.

I counseled him that it's dangerous to attempt to bring correction from a context where one stands to benefit financially from the correction.

Additionally, I advised him that it is the decision of the church board (which usually includes the pastor) to make tough decisions about the use of church finances and that he has a limited voice into such matters — it's not part of the weight that he is called to carry.

Although all three examples above help illustrate the range of perspectives on submission we face in the church, we will now focus on the issues raised by the third example as most pertinent to our discussion. We're talking here about someone who is actively involved in church leadership, but is unknowingly struggling with submission. This church leader lives in agony. He sincerely misunderstands the purpose of submission as a lifestyle and is living a life of engaged resistance to submission. Submission for him has become a series of traumatic events. My heart aches for him because I have been there and I know how miserable it feels.

Submission: Event or Lifestyle?

The concept of submission is most difficult for those who treat submission as an event rather than a lifestyle. To view submission as an event is to consider that every point of disagreement with authority requires a new decision of whether or not to be submitted. To view submission as a lifestyle is to rest in the understanding that authority is intended as a blessing and allows us to enjoy the freedom of not having to worry about some decisions. To the extent that we view submission as an event, we choose a life of anxiety. To the extent that we view submission as a lifestyle, we choose a life of peace.

Another way of describing submission as an event is that it is trying to appear submitted without being submitted because of the underlying pattern of resistance. Living this way is exhausting. If we insist on clarifying the terms of submission every time we face a disagreement with authority, we will exhaust ourselves and our leaders. It's such hard work to again and again have to evaluate the worthiness of the leader and every decision or direction a leader presents or initiates. In an effort to exhaust ourselves of bitterness, resentment and insecurity, we actually exhaust ourselves of safety, security and peace.

When we approach each issue of submission as an event, each circumstance becomes a new battlefield. The surface issue may vary, although there is usually a theme, but the heart of the issue goes to the essence of submission.

The essence of submission is acknowledging the necessity and place of leaders in my life, that I need to be part of something bigger than myself. Submission as a lifestyle views the need for leadership as a critical element of my walk with Jesus, where the focus is more on my willingness to submit than the worthiness of my leader or his/her decisions.

So, what are the keys to submission as a lifestyle rather than as an event? The two root issues have to do with 1) our willingness to truly submit to anyone and 2) how we respond when there is an issue of disagreement. Let's examine these two major areas of struggle by looking at these underlying issues and the surface questions that reveal them.

Will I submit to anyone?

The first step toward a lifestyle of submission involves consideration of whether there might be anyone to whom one is willing to submit. Although scriptural instruction to submit as citizens or wives leaves limited room for selection, the instruction to submit to our leaders carries with it a lifetime of selection of our leaders. The surface question is usually presented as, "Can I submit to him/her?", but the underlying issue is, "Will I submit to anyone?"

I recall so clearly the moment when this distinction crystalized in my heart. I was not wrestling with a particular circumstance. I thought I was wrestling with a particular relationship. Actually, I was wrestling with the very concept. I suddenly saw that the issue that held me back was not trustworthiness of a particular leader, but my own unwillingness to yield that measure of influence into my life, to acknowledge that someone else had a better perspective into my life than I did.

I saw my need for a pastor. In choosing to submit, I still retain complete responsibility for and authority over my attitude and choices. What I yield is a perspective that denies my need for others; what I embrace is a perspective that declares my need for others, a significant threshhold to cross.

It may take a long time to cross such a threshhold. There are lifelong patterns to be unlearned, and more significantly, spiritual forces to be unseated. As leaders, patience and fortitude are at a premium in helping others make this crossing. What truly sustains us at times like this is remembering the grace that has been extended to us.

When we choose to submit to someone, we are responding both to that person and to God. I used to believe that God placed me in the lives of my leaders for their benefit and that my allegiance was solely to Him. How wrong I was. God uses leaders to change us, not simply to accomplish the task or cause we signed up to support. Additionally, when we choose to submit it is important to remember that servanthood does not define its terms of service.

The major prerequisite to submission is trust. We can only submit to someone that we trust, so another restraint on our willingness to submit is our willingness and ability to trust. A common objection is a willingness to trust God, but an unwillingness to trust a person. But if I can trust God, then I can also trust Him to use the authority in my life to bless me, not abuse me.

A primary way to avoid abusive authority is to look for those who are submitted. One of the primary ways a leader cultivates trust is by living in submission. Clearly, only those in submission have authority. My strongest counsel is never to submit to someone that is not submitted.

Yet, we must not expect or demand perfection from our leaders. They are human beings doing their best to lead us. I recall so clearly a time when I was evaluating my leader. Ostensibly, my focus was on the trustworthiness of my leader, but actually I was considering the imperfection of my leader. Unknowingly, I was erecting an impossible standard, a convenient barrier to ever truly being submitted. Instead, my focus must be on the perfection of the One to whom both I and my leader are submitted.

A lifestyle of submission is tested when one is tempted to believe that one's leader stands in the way of one's progress, yet the truth remains that one's leader is most likely the way, rather than in the way. I cut off insight into my life if I retain the right or responsibility to evaluate and then accept or reject the insight of my leader.

To fully release that insight, I must believe that the one to whom I am submitted has a better perspective than I do, not simply that I am resigned to supporting that perspective. I must believe that my leader can see things that I can't see and accept what he/she says even if I don't agree, i.e. I must accept things that I don't understand, and that's the essence of faith. I can't wait to agree with things only after I understand them.

My favorite picture of submission comes courtesy of my wife. Living a life of submission is like being a sailboat, with my leader as the wind. If I fight the wind, I will capsize (event submission). If I sail with the wind, I will progress (lifestyle submission). Two clear choices, and the wise choice is obvious. I also have the option of taking down my sail and/or relocating to another bay, but of course then I would simply have to face the same issues in my life elsewhere.

There's nothing quite like the pointed reminder, via either the Holy Spirit or my wife (ususally both), "Are you fighting the wind?"

What if he/she makes the wrong decision?

The second major issue involved in a lifestyle of submission has to do with how one responds to disagreement. The surface question is usually presented as, "What if I disagree?", but the underlying issue is, "What if he/she makes the wrong decision?"

There are at least two erroneous premises in this question. One is to assume that there is a "right" or "wrong" decision. The other is, supposing that there is indeed a "right" decision, that the person in submission is in a place to make that judgement. The whole premise of submission is living under a covering and acknowledging a perspective that one doesn't have, so to wrestle with the "rightness" of the decision completely removes one from the covering.

Yet to the person living with a distorted view of submission, this contradiction isn't clear. So each new decision or direction that comes along potentially becomes another submission event, an exercise in resistance, both internal and external. Internal resistance is the struggle to somehow submit to this decision and resolve yet again to pursue the relationship of submission. External resistance is the attempt to convince the leader of a different perspective.

Disagreement is a fact of life. Disagreement with authority is guaranteed. The quality of our lives and the genuineness of our submission is not measured in terms of avoiding disagreement, it is measured in terms of how we respond to it. Event submission treats each disagreement as a contest and actually looks for opportunities to contend. Lifestyle submission, on the other hand, although free to express itself, puts its energy into teamwork, not competition.

Submission does not preclude offering different points of view. In fact, wise leadership invites the sharing of different perspectives. Leaders who understand submission are not threatened by questions, whether sincere or antagonistic. They recognize the value of listening to different points of view and strengthening or changing their original point of view.

A primary issue here has to do with motivation of the person asking the question. It is so easy for the leader to distinguish a question based on accusation from a question based on humility. If we are frustrated and angry, feeling neglected or abused, it may be because we started with the wrong motive. If I am entirely convinced of my perspective, that disables me from asking a question in humility. In the absence of a true relationship of submission, the leader has no place from which to offer instruction or bring correction, both of which are so sorely needed in our lives. We make a huge mistake when we remove ourselves from the voice of authority.

We must not be surprised when our leaders don't respond to our accusations and complaints. When our reasonings and suggestions are influenced by our feelings of resentment and bitterness, we come to poor conclusions.

Submission does involve sharing one's point of view and then resting in the decision of the leader. Peace must be found in the full expression of one's ideas and not the subsequent compliance of leadership. When the decision or direction of leadership is contrary to one's counsel (and this is a common occurence), then submission is tested.

We want to follow God's word and submit to our leaders, yet sometimes their decisions leave us with feelings of anxiety or uneasiness. What to do then? Our natural inclination is to take a stand or declare a warning, trying to make sure our leaders don't make a mistake. The truth is that we are actually safer sharing in the consequences of our leader's mistakes than we are suffering the consequences of selectively withdrawing from the covering of our leaders. (Of course, there are the horrific exceptions we are all aware of, but again those are not the sort of situations we are dealing with here.)

Sometimes instead of expressing disagreement or even after we have expressed it, we may still harbor disagreeement. I used to imagine that submission only required that I support a decision whether or not I agreed with it, but that I was allowed to retain my disagreement. What I'm learning is that the act of submission in this case is to release my disagreement and to adopt the decision as my own.

This is not an act of hypocrisy; it's an act of unity. To release our disagreement is not an act of irresponsibility, forfeiting our vigilance by not "making sure" our authority makes the "right" decision. On the contrary, it is an act of responsibililty and humility. It puts another first. It acknowledges our limitations. It promotes working together. It prioritizes relationship over opinion, a concept to be developed later.

When we care more about accomplishing a given project than our authority does, to the extent that we extend ourselves beyond the boundaries given us, then we are not submitted. That is, if our authority tells us to let something go, but we hold on to it, we're not enjoying the blessing of authority in our lives.

When we ask questions and cling to expectations of what the answer must be, then we are not submitted.

When I don't rest in the decision of my leader then I am open to all sorts of rebellious voices. Bitterness and resentment will keep gnawing away, "Why does he keep doing this?" Condescension and patronization will say, "Someday he'll wake up and do it right...my way!" Subversion and betrayal will threaten, "Show him it won't work. Don't let him do it."

Once the course is clear, once the decision is made, then lifestyle submission rests. Once one's heart is spoken, there is no need to justify one's perspective. Event submission keeps pressing, insisting it should have been done another way, or trying to open a debate on whether it was the right decision. One of the reasons we cling to disagreement may be because we simply don't want someone else telling us what to do.

One of the greatest barriers to submission in our lives is being concerned about whether or not we're being treated fairly. This is another example of viewing submission as an event rather than a lifestyle. Peace in my life can never rest on whether I'm being treated fairly or not, (which is not for me to decide). Peace in my life rests on me accepting the role that Jesus has for me.

Lifestyle submission recognizes that there are some decisions which are beyond the individual's scope and rest solely with the leader. That's part of the limited weight we are called to carry.

To repeat, when my response to a decision or direction of leadership is disagreement, that is when my submission is tested. If disagreement persists, then here's the acid test — is my disagreement founded in opinion or conscience? The key here is not to confuse opinion with conscience. It is easy to characterize disagreements as matters of conscience, but under closer scrutiny, rarely is the dispute an issue of conscience or violation of scripture.

If the disagreement is founded in opinion (and it always has been for me), it's time to decide to sacrifice the opinion on the altar of relationship rather than to sacrifice the relationship on the altar of opinion; in other words, to release the opinion in order to preserve the relationship,

If the disagreement is founded in conscience (and it never has been for me), then it's time to seriously consider releasing the relationship to preserve one's conscience. Relationship comes before opinion, but conscience comes before relationship. If it is a matter of conscience, then it may be time to remove myself from the relationship and choose someone else to which to submit.

Let's focus the issue with two questions: 1) Is this a leader to whom God has called me to submit? 2) Will I submit to the latest decision of my leader? Event submission continually focuses on the latter question, but lifestyle submission is so settled with the answer to the first question that the second one rarely comes into play.

Removing oneself from being in submission is a treacherous decision, and should only come after severe consideration of the peril of being unsubmitted, but should be accompanied by the peace of knowing God is repositioning. In this situation, there are three options: 1) Will I continue to submit myself to my leader? 2) Will I remove myself from my leader's authority and submit to another? 3) Will I live out of submission? The first two responses are equally legitimate, the third is not.

The option chosen depends ultimately on the individual and it comes down to the difference between unrighteous authority and righteous authority. Unrighteous authority uses others to promote itself and to its own advantage. Righteous authority offers itself to promote others and suffers on their behalf. This distinction is usually readily apparent and available to those who are genuinely pursuing Jesus. We rely on the grace of God and acknowledge that most issues of submission reside in the heart of the person called to submit.

Conclusion: Seven Keys to Submission as a Lifestyle

1) I am called to be a joy to my leaders, to offer everything within me and to do everything within my power to make their leadership experience a joyful one.

2) So many conflicts revolve around opinions and not around truth. Relationships are more important than opinions. I must continually remember to sacrifice my opinions for the sake of relationship and not to sacrifice relationships for the sake of my opinions.

3) The leader of a group has a perspective that no else has. His/her vision is broader and more penetrating than that of anyone else in the group. Having submitted to the leader, I trust that God has appointed him/her and speaks to and through him/her. When it comes to matters of direction, revelation, purpose and insight, his/her view is primary, to be accepted and honored.

4) There are times when my leader is looking for feedback and other times when he/she isn't, both in the sense of initial response and in the sense of ongoing counsel. My role as a servant is to be sensitive to that. My role as a student is learn from that.

5) The opinions of the leader of a group carry more weight than the opinions of others. His/her desires should be implemented whenever possible, without objection. When it comes to matters of opinion and style, every effort should be made to carry out his/her wishes.

6) The ultimate service I can perform on behalf of my leaders is to pray for them. When I feel uneasy or concerned, my initial and major response is to intercede, not to interrupt, intervene or intercept.

7) God gives me leaders because I need them and they are a blessing and a gift to me. The point is to enjoy my leaders and be grateful for them, not to resist or resent. A leader's role in my life is not dependent on my evaluation; it's dependent on God's appointment. Although there is an element of my choosing to follow, that element is preceded by my leader's choosing to lead and both choices are made in the grander design of God's plans and purposes.

Miscellaneous

They also realize that they didn't create the relationship, that there isn't a responsibility on the leader to make sure that people submit.

We can attempt to partition our lives into those portions that are submitted and those portions that are not. Additionally, we can limit the completeness of submission of those portions.

Abuse is a topic much — considered, and, not to minimize the genuine devastation that already exists and continues to be perpretrated at an alarming rate, I sometimes wonder, possibly a topic much-revered.

There can be peace without justice. Jesus accomplished peace as the object of the greatest injustice in history. Peace in my life is a consequence of living in righteously-ordered relationships, not in working to make sure my authority treats me fairly. It's hard for us to make decisions in areas where we stand to benefit from the results.

When we choose not to submit, we carry a weight and cling to anxiety that is not intended for us.

The key distinction here has to do with temporary or permanent withdrawal from submission.

Another term for temporary withdrawal is rebellion or disobedience.

When we resist authority, we embrace such an unhealthy...

The choice is clear. Either we embrace disagreement as a lifestyle and experience submission as an event or we embrace submission as a lifestyle and experience disagreement as an event.

How do we teach people how to submit without impure motives?

One reason there are degrees of submission is because there are degrees of trust. Trust is cultivated by the leader. The more trust the leader cultivates, the more submission he/she reaps.

What are the most common techniques employed by the person who is trying to be submitted without being submitted?

Self-justification: When you know that no good can come from your response, but you want to make sure they know that I know that I'm right.

Insecurity: We want to do something because we decide to and not because asked to

What comes first: understanding or experience, i.e. Can we understand submission without experiencing it? Can we experience submission without understanding it? The answer to both questions is yes, because there are degrees

*** Accepting things we do not yet understand is the essence of faith. To retain the expectation of achieving understanding is not dishonest or hypocritical, as long as one is willing to lay it down and not use it as either a sword or a shield. but that expectation must be held loosely.

Here are a series of questions to help us in evaluating both the authenticity and effectiveness of our submission.

Submission releases faith. Jesus issued His greatest affirmation of faith in response to a statement regarding authority and submission. (Matthew 8)

*** It is easy to confuse submission with a variety of other attitudes: suppression, resentment, denial, dominance.

*** We do not convince people to submit to us, but as leaders it is our responsibility teach them about the blessings of living in submission and the dangers of living out of submission.

There is simply no point in fighting the wind. True, the analogy only works with the feature that I can

You can lead without discipling, but you can't disciple without leading.

One of the greatest barriers to growth in the local church is the unwillingness of those involved to submit. The most obvious target is the (Senior) Pastor. So many church splits are the result of an unwillingness to submit, placing one's opinions ahead of one's relationships. There are always competing views lying around in various stages of development waiting for a catalyst. The members of the leadership team possess the capacity for uniting the forces of change or fueling the fire of separation.

There is a well-documented list of growth barriers, but one of the greatest threats to growth is the "church split".

Scenarios:

*Sitting in the living room realizing that the issue was whether I could submit to anyone

*Going on the mission trip and immediately encountering someone speaking to me about requiring perfection in our leaders. Certainly there are ways to distort — balance lies between disparaging and deifying. If we disparage than we are only pretending to submit. If deify, then we have gone beyond submission...

*Discussion of tension in our relationship where the roles got confused. From his perspective, we were learning to work together. From my perspective, I was learning how to submit.

Submission is not a substitute for working together — it's actually an element of working together.

Please know that I continue to be a willing ear and whether or not my comments are helpful to you, I thank you for the opportunity to share them with a fellow minister who is willing to face the tough issues.

A PASTOR'S PLACE
IN THE LIFE OF PEOPLE

David M. Edwards

Recently I have been more spiritually aware than ever before as to the place a pastor holds in the hearts and lives of people. Pastoring is an Office Gift that is given by Jesus Christ to the Church for the equipping of the saints to train them to do the work of the ministry. Pastoring is also synonymous with shepherding and all of the imagery that that brings to our minds, i.e., protector, keeper of the gate, scare away the wolves, seek out the lost sheep and bring them to the fold, the rod and staff, etc. Pastoring does mean feeding the flock and providing a well-balanced diet of the Word of God on an ongoing basis. Pastoring means leading by example and living a life that is circumspect and godly. All of these things I knew when I was called to be a pastor. But I never quite figured out the role that I played in people's lives. I mean, what is it that I do that means so much to them or how important are the words I use and to what degree does it shape their lives?

I Remember When

I remember growing up in church and having pastors that were larger than life itself. To me they represented what God must be like and act and feel. I was raised to respect and revere anyone in the ministry. I was also raised to not talk against anyone in the ministry. The pastors that I had, had a profound impact on my life and my spiritual journey. To this day I can quote many things that were said by my former pastors. If I were to see any one of them today I would immediately address them as Pastor so and so. But oh how I've forgotten all of that.

It's hard for me to see what others see in me. I tend to see the negative, the bad, the things that need fixing and the things that need to change. But they hardly see all of that. Like it or not, you are to them larger than life. How you respond to them, how you treat them, and how you minister to them will be remembered for a life time. That's kind of scary if you ask me. "That's too much responsibility," I remember telling the Lord when He called me into this thing called pastoring. And that's just it — I didn't choose to be a pastor. In fact, I vowed I would never be one — so much for never. He chose me, and that at times is a lot to think about. He chose me, and every other pastor, to intersect the lives of people to affect them with Good News, with healing, with pure love, and true life. And as a result, God has given pastors a special place in the hearts of those they serve. A place that is privileged and yet a place that I, as a pastor, must guard and see as a sacred trust.

Just as those pastors were a channel of God's grace to me growing up, I in turn must allow myself to become a channel of God's grace to those who are learning and growing around me. They will remember what I do and say for a long time and I want to make it count — every word, every action, every attitude in my heart toward them, I want to make it count!

A Larger Than Life Calling

We are products of our environments for sure. I believe that my spiritual environment has been healthy and whole to a large degree because of my godly parents, but also because of men and women who ministered to my spiritual needs and to this day are larger than life to me. We tend to believe, "they don't make 'em like they used to..." Well, I have to admit that at times I've thought that about certain things, including church leaders, and yet God's call to every pastor is to be like Him. God is still making and molding people like He always has. God is still giving pastors a larger than life broadcast into the lives of men and women. And I've finally figured out that it's not the pastor whose larger than life, it's the pastoral office itself that's larger than life. I'm not larger than life, but what God has called me to do is way beyond me — larger than anything I could ever attempt to do in the flesh. Pastoring would be and is a failure without His help, His anointing, His gifting, and His grace. Men and women need something that's bigger than themselves, something that's bigger than this life, and pastors represent that to them. A voice of hope amidst the negative energy of their day, a healing hand in a crowd of so many with tight fists, a forgiving spirit when it's popular to be a victim, etc. Any God-called ministry is larger than life because there's nothing in this life without Him that could ever change a thing!

A Place Of Value

A pastor's place in the lives of those he or she serves is a place of value. Yes, value! People want relationships that are worth something — there's value to them. And people seek the same thing in a pastor. They gave them a place of value because of the worth they feel from the ministry they receive. Someone told me recently following one of our Sunday morning services, "you'll never know how much you mean to me..." At first I thought how nice that was of them to say that and my second thought was that most pastors probably don't realize how much they do mean to people.

I'm even talking about people that barely know you and even they can feel valued because of your ministry touching them in some way even through other people, i.e., lay leaders, staff, home group leaders, etc. It's an amazing thing to me that someone who doesn't even know me can come up to me and say, "you have touched our lives in so many ways." And you're thinking, "boy, I have? How?" Therein lies the interesting thing about all of this: people can feel valued by you whether or not they know you very well or very little. This fact makes it all the more important to make sure that I am communicating clearly to our leadership our core values and what we're all about and how we go about doing kingdom stuff around here. A pastor's influence is realized well beyond the boundaries of his office door and the pulpit on the platform!

People want to have someone in their life that they can value and hold up as an example of how to live your life for Jesus Christ. Churches are still growing even after the infamous television evangelists debacle, even after famous preachers were "exposed" on evening news programs, etc. The reason is that even after all of that, people still want and need someone to value, someone to believe in, someone to live the life before them. A place of value is still given in a society that has become popular at de-valuing just about everything.

A Place Of Trust

Pastors hold a place of trust in peoples lives as well. A place where people can reveal who they really are, make themselves vulnerable, and hopefully are not disappointed in the process. As a pastor I must realize that God has entrusted me with the heart secrets of many who come into my life. People will share things with a pastor before they'll ever share them with someone else. Why? Because a pastor hold's a place of trust in the lives of people. A place where confidences can be kept, where real truth is sorted out amidst the rubble of everyday living, and where safety can be a sure thing.

More importantly though, is the fact that I must hold that trust and guard it well. I must choose my words carefully when discussing with a colleague the nature of a situation which I have been entrusted with. I must maintain personal and spiritual integrity in all my dealings. I must show mercy, grace and guidance to those whom I must lead through rough times or difficult circumstances. When someone tells me something that truly shocks me, I need to be careful that I do not become judgmental or feel spiritually superior to them because I would never do such a thing.

As a pastor you know things about people within your church that no one else will ever know. It needs to stay that way. If I feel led to share something with another person whom I think could play an important role in someone's deliverance, I will ask permission to share it from the person who needs ministry. I am reading ministry reports, receiving information from staff, and getting prayer requests all the time that require me to walk with integrity and not turn matters of concern into idle or inappropriate conversation.

For instance, if someone were to find out that the things they shared with you — that took so much courage to do, were being discussed or even made light of, it would literally destroy them and their confidence in you. Furthermore, it says about yourself that you've not learned to properly appreciate the place God's given you in someone's life and it also belittles their situation. To you it may not seem like much, but to them it may be very traumatic. Sometimes I think to myself that what this person or that person is going through seems awful silly and childish — but then I have to remember that they were not raised the way I was, they do not process life's obstacles the way I do, and my thinking that it's silly is exactly what the enemy told them I would think! I'm sure that many things have bothered me that others would be inclined to think, "how childish." But we're all growing and developing at different stages of God's grace and in our understanding of how to apply the Word of God to our situation. Even though I'm a pastor, I'm learning too and I am growing through my own weaknesses and shortcomings.

To Be Real When They See Me And When They Don't

We've all heard the often quoted saying, "who you are in private is who you'll be in public". When I get up to speak before my congregation, I want to make sure that what I am sharing about and what

I am teaching comes from my own life experiences and that I am not preaching something I'm certainly not living! I must be real. People want pastors and ministers to be real. They're tired of the fake, the hype, and the fluff. People are tired of being entertained and talked down to, etc., people are hungry for the real man or woman of God to take his or her place in the kingdom and simply be real. Don't try to be something that you're not — they'll see right through it. Don't lay claim to something that's not yours. Just be who God's made you and called you to be — that is enough challenge for anyone.

The more real that you can be with people, the greater the place you'll have in their lives. The most precious compliment that anyone can give to me is when they say, "you're real". That's when I feel like I've finally accomplished something, e.g., when I've made myself real to someone and it's helped them. A dear friend is always telling me that we must build a positive track record in someone's life in order for them to even give us the benefit of a doubt. That's so true. The whole time your ministering to some people there's this little nagging question going on in the back of their brain that says, "How long can I trust you?" or "How long until you burn me?" And what a surprise for them when you don't break their confidence and you don't burn them. After awhile they begin to say, "You know I've trusted this guy through just about everything and he's never done me wrong or lied to me". That means a lot to people especially today. I must show myself a faithful friend and confidant if I'm really going to help someone. There must be a continual revealing to them that I am who I say I am.

If I am inconsistent in my personal life, sooner or later, it will surface in my public ministry. And I also believe that God loves me enough to not allow it to go on, in other words, He will make sure it surfaces. My "ministry" to my wife and kids is intricately tied to the ministry of others. It is there, in our home, that I must first practice what I preach and give to them my very best. It is there that I must first "be real" and earn their trust and confidence first and foremost. It is up to me to keep my life clean and my heart pure. That's my responsibility and no one else's. I can blame no one else for my sin and my mistakes. If my family sees a different person at church than the one they see at home, then I am guilty of impersonating a minister and it's spiritual abuse.

Being Honest, Even If It Hurts

"Speak the truth in love..." we like to quote that verse. It's kind of funny how many times we quote it, but how few times we do it. And yes,

I am guilty of not doing it all the time. As guilty as the rest of you who are reading this. What is it about telling "the truth" , that we don't like. For me it's mostly the overwhelming feeling that if I tell someone the truth will they really like me then? Or how about when it's someone that's been around for years and years, you kind of get used to them doing their own thing even though you detest it. What is it about telling "the truth" that causes us to whence? It's because the truth hurts sometimes and we don't want to hurt them even though we know they need to hear it. We rationalize and think to ourselves that it would be better just to leave certain things alone and unbothered — but the problem is that nothing gets resolved, nothing gets healed, and no one's getting any better. That's a big dilemma for more than a few pastors.

For me personally, if I don't speak the truth to people about what is bothering me or even what the Lord is showing me, I can become cynical and sarcastic about that person and very critical. I'll get critical about their doing the very thing that God's wants me to talk to them about. But rather than confront them, there's this little lie that runs around in our heads that says, "give them time, they'll change". The problem is that it turns into months and years and your still telling yourself, "give them time, they'll change". They won't change because they don't see it like you do. They don't perceive it as part of their problem. You're agreeing with them or even staying neutral is an affirmation that what they're doing is right and spiritually healthy.

Another aspect of being honest and or "speaking the truth in love", is that there's no room in our hearts for compromise or harboring ill feelings. Getting everything above board with people help's me to not feel like I'm walking on egg-shells around someone. If we truly are concerned with the spiritual welfare of others, we will speak the truth in love. In other words, it's a truth that is spoken into the heart of someone your ministering to and after it's spoken you then show them the pathway of God's grace, forgiveness, and mercy. Big deal if we were to speak the truth to people without any avenue of escape and restoration. That is why there is no condemnation for those who are in Christ Jesus. Yes, there's conviction, but not condemnation. When sin has been properly pointed out in our lives and it's done in love, true repentance and healing follow. As a result, more of our "self" dies and more of Him comes alive in us. He works more and more of His likeness and character in us through these kinds of truthful dealings. Faithful are the wounds of a friend — and a true friend will help to clean the wound and dress it!

A Place Of Opportunity

In the giving of ministry office gifts to the Church, Jesus Christ did so in order for the Church to be equipped to do the work of ministry, that the members would thus be edified and feel fulfilled, and that we would all mature in the faith to the degree that we're in unity with one another and with Him. Pastors are given this assignment: equip people for ministry! Most churches in our country do not fulfill this God-given assignment. They don't even come close. "Why, that's what a staff is for," some might say. Or God forbid, "If I let the people do the ministry, what am I supposed to do?" What pastors are supposed to do is equip people for ministry and part of equipping them is letting them do the ministry.

People are looking for a place of opportunity. A place where they can "do" something, not just sit on the sidelines. Sure, there are those "mature" Christians who have served their apprenticeship and have "grown beyond needing to be involved in ministry..." But for the most part, people want to do something — they want to get involved. And pastors must realize that everyone has a seed to sow, a gift to give, a talent to invest, a place of service to fill, etc. God has called me to be an open door of opportunity for everyone that finds a home in this congregation. People see this office as a place of opportunity and I can't afford to disappoint them or God.

I must make room for everyone. Yes, it's a challenge. But what fun and what results! Giving people a place to serve gives them confidence and shows them that you believe in giving them an opportunity to serve. People will grow up in the Lord faster if they have a place where they can serve Him. People tend to get healed faster when they're giving of themselves in service to others. We must work against the notion that only platform personalities and church staff are "qualified" to do the work of the ministry. The quickest way to do that is to give ministry opportunities away. I don't want to do all the ministry around here and even if I did, I could never do it. It wasn't designed by God for me to do it all. A have to be a channel of opportunity for others so that they and I can mature in the faith.

Conclusion

What is it that I do that means so much to people? How important are the words I use? To what degree does it shape their lives? All of these questions surface in my mind when I think about "pastoring". I've tried to answer them to some degree. There's more to be said for sure, but as long as I keep thinking about it and examining my heart before God I'll be just fine.

CONFESSIONS OF A PHARISEE

Tom Gardner

I am a Pharisee. I hate to admit it, but I am. I like order and things to go smoothly. The externals of my life are in order. I was raised in Church. I came from a stable and healthy home with loving and supportive parents. I never went through a rebellious stage. I gave my heart to Jesus when I was six. I am a third generation Christian. All four of my grandparents made a personal commitment to Christ as adults. Because of their decision, I stand apart from the very trauma that brought them face to face with the realization that their lives weren't working and that they needed Jesus. Their relationship with Christ revolutionized their lives and set them on a solid course of which I am a benefactor. Sociologists call this process redemption and lift. Almost all sovereign moves of God begin amongst the masses; people whose lives are destroyed by the reality of a fallen world. As they allow the redemptive work of the Holy Spirit in their lives, they become part of the classes and are removed from the factors that compelled them to give their lives to Christ. This kind of environment is conducive to producing Pharisees - people's lives that appear to work, at least externally, but are devoid of love and grace. As a Pharisee, I can be critical and judgmental of people whose lives are shattered by the ravages of sin and need to know the love of God changing their life.

In the recent past, we saw a generation of unwashed hippies committed to tearing down the establishment exchange their rainbow painted VWs for glistening BMWs; illegal drugs for prescription drugs. These anti-establishment types have now become the establishment. One only has to look at the stark contrast between the Woodstock of 1969 and the Woodstock of 1994 to see the truth of this statement.

A Pharisee, then, can be produced in any Church, in any Christian home. The order and stability can foster external adherence to the principles of the Gospel without changing the internals. If we are not careful, we end up producing "career Christians," people who know about God but don't know God - in other words, modern day Pharisees. Paul warned Timothy to beware of those "*having the form of godliness but denying its power*," (2 Timothy 3:5). If we are not careful, our children never progress past a second grade Sunday School class view of God instead of a life changing experience with Jesus. Jerry Cook, noted author, once taught that we can actually inoculate people against the truth. We pass on a dead "virus" of religiosity that builds up an immunity to the truth. When a person comes in contact with the real Christianity, they reject it as irrelevant and do not investigate it.

But wait a minute, does such a narrow view of Pharisees miss something important? And, can God use a Pharisee?

To do this topic justice, we need a short review of who the Pharisees were and the socio-political and religious climate of the period which we are most familiar; the New Testament era. Because of the intense upheaval of the inter-testimental period, Judaism of the time had fractured into four main groups: the Sadducees, the Zealots, the Essenes, and the Pharisees.

The Sadducees played a large role in the period before, during, and immediately after Jesus came to earth. Because they did not believe in a resurrection of the dead (and therefore an eternal judgment), life was all about the here and now. They threw in their lot with the Roman rulers. The Sadducees controlled the Sanhedrin, which explains much of the events surrounding the crucifixion and the Book of Acts. Caiaphas, concerned for the political stability of the nation prophesied of Jesus, "*It is good that one man should die for the people*," (John 11:50). Jesus and His message did not fit the world view of the Sadducees and so they endeavored to silence Him by nailing Him to a cross. They didn't count on the resurrection or an empty tomb. Even though they fought against God, His eternal purposes were not thwarted by men. Because of their pragmatic and secular stance, a person concerned for doing the will of God can easily reject the model of the Sadducees as a pattern for living life.

The Zealots, another of the Jewish factions, took an opposing view from that of the Sadducees. They hated Rome with a passion and were dedicated to the violent overthrow of the hated oppressors. They committed themselves to humanly ushering in the Kingdom of God. For them, the end justified the means. They could not grasp the spiritual truths expressed by Jesus, "*My Kingdom is not of this world*," (John 18:36). Some portions of the contemporary Church could fall into this same rationale today if they endeavor to build the Kingdom by human effort.

The next group was the Essenes, the people who produced the Dead Sea Scrolls. They were an eschatological community consumed with the coming Messianic Age when good would finally conquer evil. They simply opted out of the fallen, evil, material world. By removing themselves from society, they removed themselves from influencing society. Perhaps the modern day equivalent of these people are those who are "so heavenly minded that they are of no earthly good." (For me, this represents an oxymoron. To be heavenly minded is to be of great earthly good. No one was more heavenly minded than Jesus and no one made a greater impact for good on earth than Jesus).

So, that brings us to the Pharisees. Unlike the Sadducees, they did believe in a resurrection of the dead and that one day, they would be required to stand before a holy God to give an account. Birthed in the crucible of the Babylonian Exile, they had to look for something more. Jerusalem lay in ruins: the Temple was destroyed. No longer were sacrifices offered daily upon the altar. Worshipping God had to be more than the externals of the Temple worship. They found solace in the study of the Torah. They embraced the conviction that faith in God had to translate into the actions of everyday life. (Here I identify with the Pharisees unashamedly because I share this conviction). To this end, they codified their teaching on almost every subject imaginable in several compendia of material: the Talmud, the Mishnah, and the Halakah. But in their zeal to serve God, they made the terrible mistake of thinking that rules and regulations could change the heart. (The truth is that outward change proceeds from a changed heart). What began as a spiritual response to a changing world over time degenerated into mere form and ritual.

To further complicate things, they developed a tradition that Moses received an Oral Law on Mt. Sinai that was of equal authority to the Written Law. It was this Oral Law (traditions of the Fathers) that brought Jesus into direct conflict with the Pharisees of His day. Matthew 15:1 - 19 records such a face-off. Some of the Pharisees and teachers of the Law challenged Jesus on the fact that His disciples did not wash their hands before eating and thus broke the tradition of the Elders. Jesus used this occasion to teach that the human heart was what mattered to God. He went as far as calling them hypocrites. (A hypocrite has nothing to do with perfection but everything to do with pretending to be something he or she is not). Jesus quoted Isaiah,

> *These people honor me with their lips, but their hearts are farfrom me. They worship me in vain; their teachings are but rulestaught by men,* (Mt. 15:8 - 9; cp. Is. 29:13).

Jesus never violated the Written Law. In fact, He went so far as to say that He came not to abolish the Law but to fulfill it, (Mt. 5:12). Jesus embodied the spirit of the Law. The Law was all about loving God with your whole heart and loving your neighbor, (cp. Mt. 22:34 - 40). Many of the Pharisees, then and now, just didn't get it. Matthew 9:9 - 13 records another exchange between Jesus and the Pharisees that brings this into sharp focus. They quizzed Jesus' disciples as to why He associated with sinners. Jesus quickly cut to the heart of the matter. *"It is not the healthy who need a doctor, but the sick. But go and learn what this means: ' desire mercy, not sacrifice.' For I have not come to call the righteous, but sinners, "* (Mt. 9:12 - 13). Understanding the tension between being true to the spirit of the Law or keeping the letter of the Law is the secret to resolving the conflict for people like me who tend to be Pharisees and yet desire to touch the lost world in life.

Up until this point, we have focused primarily upon the negative aspects of Pharisaism. To be fair, a few things need to be said in their defense. The Pharisees were not all wrong. No one lived more externally like Jesus. They were clean living people that paid fastidious attention to the smallest detail of walking in righteousness. They understood the importance of discipleship. Because of this, as was said earlier, they developed a systematic approach to making disciples. They were concerned with stability and sustainability. They understood from experience that emotion could only take a person so far. We see the strength of their conviction demonstrated in this century as Jews marched toward the gas chambers drawing strength by repeating the Shema, *"Hear O Israel, the Lord our God is one Lord,"* (Deut. 6:4).

Their great strengths, however, became their greatest weakness. Their clean living made them intolerant of the very people who needed what they had to offer. As you recall, that was God's plan, that His chosen people would be a light to the nations. Unfortunately, the Jews developed an "us" and "them" mentality that built almost insurmountable walls between themselves and those who needed God's love and light. (Before we get too smug and righteously indignant, I see a similar thing manifesting itself within the contemporary Church). Their attention to detail drove them to *"strain at a gnat and swallow a camel,"* (Mt. 23:24). They tithed on mint and cumin while neglecting the weightier things like love and mercy (Mt. 23:23). In other words, they were lacking in heart.

Their clean living created another problem; that of self-righteousness. (Self-righteousness, like cynicism is a religious occupational disease). They ordered their lives so well that they outgrew their need of God's spirit working redemptively in their lives. For them, slavish attention to the rules was good enough. They became religious to make up for the lack of personal relationship with God. The sad thing was, they were not even aware of the problem.

The Pharisaism that Jesus denounced, and the religious spirit so destructive today, concerns itself with externals. Appearances are everything. Jesus addressed this over and over in His diatribes directed at the Pharisees. They prayed long prayers. They loved to be seen by others; all the while being unaware of their spiritual bankruptcy. Jesus likened them to white washed tombs; beautiful on the outside but full of death inside.

Nowhere is this more clearly illustrated than in the story of the Pharisee and the Publican praying in the Temple. The Pharisee rehearsed his good deeds and self-righteousness, thanking God that he was not like the Publican. The Publican, on the other hand, recognized his unworthiness and pleaded for God's mercy. Jesus posed the rhetorical question, *"Which man went away justified?"* (Luke 18:9 - 14).

All too often, I see the Pharisee in me when I am confronted with non-Churched people or when I hear of worship forms different from my own. I see the negatives: All too often I am critical and judgmental, applying my standards and lifestyle to people who did not have the same choices that I did. (My hope is that my recognition of this can help me not to duplicate the negatives of being a Pharisee in my life and ministry). When I hear of new and different things that God is doing, I can all too easily dismiss something that may be good because it does not conform to my concepts of how God works. And, if I am not careful, I could miss God, just like the First Century Pharisees.

They missed Jesus because they were looking for someone else (John 1:12). Instead of a prince born in a palace, Jesus came as a babe in a stable. Instead of a conquering hero to lead them in battle against the Romans, Jesus came as a suffering servant who went to a cruel cross to defeat the spiritual oppressor. Could we miss what God wants to do because we aren't expecting Him to move in a new way? We read that the Pharisees and the people of the day literally tied the hands of Christ. Matthew 13:58 records that Jesus could not do many mighty things in His own town because of their unbelief. They put God in a box and said, "You can't do that - you can't work that way!" What is the contemporary equivalent of "you can't heal on the Sabbath?" Could my Pharisee attitude block the move of the Spirit? The obvious answer and it implications are sobering to say the least.

We all give lip service to allowing God to move, but when He does, will we be open to this move? In the last great awakening of the 70's, some embraced what God was doing while others did not. Will we be Pharisees or will we be willing to negotiate the excesses on both sides? Revivals are messy. I once heard Roy Hicks, Jr. say "Don't pray for revival unless you are willing to pray lots and stay up nights." Once again, we find ourselves between two tension points: structure and freedom. Too much structure and we restrict the flow of the Holy Spirit. Too much freedom and we risk chaos, the works of the flesh, or even worse, manifestations of the demonic.

What brought this whole issue of being a Pharisee into sharp focus for me is a spiritual stirring presently taking place here in Canada. Last spring, we began to hear reports that "revival had broken out" in Toronto, Ontario, and we rejoiced because, unlike the United States, Canada has never had a national spiritual awakening. Side on with the encouraging news, however, were reports that also troubled me: uncontrolled laughter that left people powerless on the floor, people of slurred speech who were "drunk in the Spirit." (The August 1994 *Charisma* magazine chronicles similar occurrences taking place in the United States.) Immediately, a million thoughts bombarded my brain. I asked (and continue to ask) myself, "Am I so inflexible or is there legitimate cause for concern?" "Do they have the necessary safeguards in place?" (cp. 1 Cor. 12 - 14). "Are they going beyond what is written?" (1 Cor. 4:6). "Are we in danger of chasing after signs and wonders instead of having signs and wonders follow us?"

Don't get me wrong, I am not saying that what is taking place cannot be genuine. The accounts of past awakenings mention similar occurrences; people shaking uncontrollably, and falling down under the power of God. I think most notably of the Weslyan revival of the 1700's. This event revolutionized the society; bars closed, people's lives were forever changed. Is that happening in this awakening or are people looking for a spiritual high or to get "zapped"? By the way, the Weslyans moved to stabilize and sustain the move of God by introducing a methodical approach to personal devotions - hence the name Methodists. Are those who are part of this present move critical of this kind of mid-course correction and becoming Pharisees, too?

We should not be surprised that Jesus had to address the problem of people's motivation for following Him, too. John 6 is a watershed of Jesus' ministry here on earth. As you recall, Jesus fed the 5000. After this miraculous multiplication, Jesus withdrew. The crowd pursued Him across the lake. They sought after Him not because He had the Words of life but because their bellies were full. Their focus was in the wrong place. *"Unless you are willing to eat my flesh and drink my blood,"* Jesus said, *"you have no life in you,"* (John 6:53). The spectacular, the miraculous are wonderful, but neither is the main issue. The issue is following Christ. Does this sound like the statement of a Pharisee? To some, it might. Jesus communicated in word and deed that following

God's commands would mean hard work, and even equated keeping His commandments with truly loving Him, (John 14:15).

A spiritual, mystical touch from God, then, must be followed with teaching. The Pharisees, at least at some point, understood this, and so must we. As a person with a strong teaching gift, I am dedicated to the second half of the Great Commission, *"...teaching them to obey everything I have commanded you,"* (Mt. 28:20). Jesus was concerned about grounding people, too. Notice He commissioned His disciples to pass on what He had taught them. I desire for people to be firmly grounded in their faith and know how to walk. If that makes me a Pharisee, then in this case, I wear the title proudly.

The problem of the Pharisees in Jesus' day was not in their desire to teach but that their teaching had lost its relevance and its power; in large measure because of the things we have already discussed. The crowds noticed the difference in Jesus' teaching. At the conclusion of the Sermon on the Mount, Matthew includes their review. *"The crowds were amazed at his teaching, because he taught as one who had authority, and not as their teachers of the law,"* (Mt. 7:28 - 29). Jesus' teaching cut to the very quick of their existence. He gave them answers, not catechism learned by rote. After years of teaching the basic principles of the Kingdom of God, could I become so rigid and brittle in my preaching that I lose the new wine of current revelation because of my personal need for order?

The Apostle Paul becomes an excellent role model for how God can and will use a Pharisee. Paul epitomizes the truth of what Jesus said in Matthew 13:52, *"Every teacher of the law who has been instructed about the Kingdom of heaven is like the owner of a house who brings out of his storeroom new treasures as well as old."* In his personal testimony, Saul (Paul) confessed that he was a Pharisee, the son of a Pharisee; according to the law blameless. His zeal for his traditions led him to violently persecute the Church, thus fulfilling Gamaliel's warning, *"In the present case I advise you: Leave these men alone!...For if their purpose or activity is of human origin, it will fail. But if it is from God, you will not be able to stop these men; you will only find yourself fighting against God,"* (Acts 5:38-39). Paul kept the law but was missing the essential ingredient - heart (love). Jesus Himself appeared to Paul on the Damascus road. That encounter revolutionized his life. He still lived a very disciplined life, but now he had something more - the Spirit.

Paul duplicated the godly lifestyle in his disciples and in the churches he planted. *"I am sending you Timothy, my son whom I love, who is faithful in the Lord. He will remind you of my way of life in Christ Jesus, which agrees with what I teach everywhere in every church, "* (1 Cor. 4:16 - 17).

All of Paul's learning was not wasted. God used Paul mightily as the champion of salvation by faith. The Pharisee Paul had learned about a righteousness that was not derived from the Law. He used his vast knowledge about the Scriptures to argue that Jesus was the promised Messiah and then to defend the doctrine of salvation by grace.

After mulling all of this over, I have arrived at the conclusion that a pastor's concerns are very much like those of the Pharisees of the New Testament. Pastors (and Pharisees) are concerned about their people's stability and growth. The Apostle Paul wrote to his churches with explicit instructions about how to live. He also chided some of them for not progressing past the milk of the Word stage. Pastors (and Pharisees) are concerned with protecting the flock. A good shepherd cares about the sheep. One way to protect is to make sure the flock feeds in green pastures and besides still waters, away from the hazards of excesses along the way.

Protecting, like most concepts of this paper, is both good and bad. Protecting is good when our motives are pure and directed toward the best interests of others and doing the will of God. Protecting is bad when our hearts and motives are not correct. The Pharisees of Jesus' day were protecting their vested interests. For them to change meant giving up their position and power. I ask myself, what vested interest do I have that might block me from allowing God to move?

Pastors (and Pharisees) are concerned about sustainability. As my earthly father often reminds me, life is a marathon, not a sprint. It is not he who starts fast but he who finishes that is the true victor. Paul continually talks in terms of endurance - endure hardship, run the race, discipline yourself for the purpose of godliness, keep the flesh under control. In our Foursquare Movement, we have examples of revivals that have been sustained - Hope Chapel, Church on the Way, and Faith Center in Eugene to name a few. All of these churches benefited from the sovereign move of God during the Jesus Revolution of the late '60's and early '70's. All three remain vital today and continue to train leaders and birth churches.

Jesus, too, was concerned with sustainability. He warned His followers to be on guard when difficult times would come and that even the very elect might be deceived. He challenged them that following Him would not be easy and that being His disciple would mean death to self. His earthly ministry was (and is) more than a dog and pony show. It had substance. It had heart. The supernatural provided the attesting miracles that helped to substantiate His claim to be God's Messiah. But for His disciples to endure, they had to have a view of who He really was.

The Transfiguration helps us see all of these elements, the supernatural, obedience and sustainability, in proper balance. Jesus took Peter, James, and John up a mountain to pray. Once there, the Father revealed Jesus in heavenly splendor. The Bible records that the disciples fell to the ground. (One could argue that they were "slain in the spirit," i.e. could not remain standing because of the awesome power of God). Jesus knew that they needed to see Him as He really was if they were to survive seeing Him on the cross and persevere until the post-resurrection appearances. In the blinding light of the transfiguration, we often overlook one vital component; the words of the Father, *"This is My Son...listen to Him,"* (Mt. 17:5). Peter responded to the whole situation as I see many people around me responding to the spectacular. He wanted to stay on the mountain top. But Jesus had (has) a different idea. The disciples had to leave that wondrous place, descend from the mountain, and share what they had seen and heard.

To present Jesus accurately, we cannot deny the supernatural. Well educated and strong minded people often struggle with the supernatural and yet Jesus, the New Testament, and the Gospels cannot be fairly presented without things that are beyond the natural. I am sure that the Pharisees looked on the earthly ministry of Jesus in a similar manner to how modern Pharisees look at various "moves of God" that come down the pike. Jesus' earthly ministry blazed across the spiritual night of the First Century AD like some glorious comet lighting the sky. Large crowds thronged to hear this Jesus of Nazareth. Miracles and supernatural events punctuated His earthly ministry. Blind eyes were opened; deaf ears unstopped. He even raised the dead. And don't tell me that you haven't struggled with Jesus' forcible expulsion of the moneychangers from the Temple. In the understatement of the year, not everyone was happy. Even members of His immediate family, including His mother, were uncomfortable with His presentation, (Mk. 3:21, 31-35). I wonder what they wished to speak with Him about? Do you suppose they said things like, "Are you okay? Do you really know what you are doing? Maybe you have been in the sun too long?"

Pharisees, then and now, don't like change. And after all, isn't protecting all about keeping the *status quo*? Again, Jesus warned about rejecting the new wine for the old sweet wine that was "good enough," (Luke 5:39). Again, I see myself. I was raised in a small town in Ohio that characterized all that was good and right about middle America in the 1960's. I am accused of growing up in "white picket fence land." Occasionally, I am asked what color the sky is in my world by people who did not have such an idyllic background. This stability gives me tremendous resources from which to draw when helping others. This stability also created an aversion for changes. And yet, to be relevant in a large urban center in the 1990's, change is not only good but essential if I hope to be relevant. (Remember, the Gospel is changeless, the methods used in sharing it are not). I must constantly guard myself from becoming resistant to the fresh wind of the Holy Spirit that refreshes both me and those I touch. Will I allow Jesus to take my past and infuse it with His Spirit? Or will I, like most of the Pharisees, allow relevance to slip past me to become hopelessly out of touch with the fallen world in which I live?

So how do I embrace the good in being a Pharisee while minimizing the bad? A starting point is having an openness to let God be God. God is a God of order, but also a God of creativity. We must not confuse creativity with chaos or lack of integrity. God will always act in a manner consistent with Himself. He will, however, act contrary to some of our pre-conceived ideas of Him. If we are not careful, we can worship our ideas and traditions, making them idols; idols as real as any image of gold or silver.

In our quest for newness, our protection against selling out is in our commitment to walking in integrity. The story of Abimelech in Genesis 20 shows us that God protects those who walk in integrity of heart from sinning against Him. A person who walks in integrity will also walk in sensitivity to the Holy Spirit. Even those who have been Christians for a long time, (especially those who have been Christians for a long time), need to cultivate an openness to the new things God desires to do. We should make sure that we are on the auto-pilot of the Holy Spirit and not the auto-pilot of our traditions.

We also need to come to grips with the spiritual truth that we don't see things the way God sees them. We tend to look only on the externals, the outward appearance of things, both good and bad. God, on the other hand, looks on the heart, the internals, (cp. 1 Sam. 16:7). His ways are higher than our ways. Our responsibility is to do what God asks of us and trust Him to take care of others who may do things differently. I am convinced that many valid ways exist to run a Church. One is not better than another as long as Jesus is at the center of all that is done.

Pharisees would tend to look at what others are doing and somehow try to make themselves feel better by being critical of others. Jesus recognized this human weakness and gave wise counsel by warning us to be careful how we judge, (Mt. 7:1 - 5). He did not say we were not to judge, He just said we needed to judge with fairness and equality because the standard we apply in our judgment will be applied to us. The best way to escape the negative trap of Pharisaism is to walk in love and walk closely with Jesus. Allow Him to deal with us, do what He says, and trust Him with other people.

John 21 brings this principle into sharp focus. After a miraculous catch of fish and breakfast, Jesus and Peter went for a walk on the beach - just the two of them. Jesus pressed Peter on the level of his personal commitment. When it began to get too hot, Peter glanced over his shoulder and noticed John following behind them just out of earshot. Peter, trying to deflect the issue asked Jesus, "And what about John?" Jesus' answer give us tremendous direction, "Let me worry about John, you follow me."

Another way of looking at the whole issue is the need for balance. And yet, even the need for balance must be balanced. Sam Rockwell, in his essay *Form and Fire: Fostering Disequilibium in the Church*,[1] made an excellent observation. He pointed out that one definition for the word equilibrium is to neutralize all opposing forces. The danger is in balancing things so well, establishing such equilibrium that no forward progress is made. We need to trust God for balance without stagnation; equilibrium without sterility. We need discipline and we need passion. We need to remember that when things go too smoothly, we don't need faith.

Being a Pharisee, then, is not all bad as long as we embrace the best of what they stood for and beware the pitfalls of crippling criticism and conformity to externals (religion) without understanding the internals (relationship with God). Negotiating these treacherous straits is essential to allowing the newness and freshness of the Holy Spirit to move in ways that might be uncomfortable for us without His order. By cultivating discernment regarding the dangers of the extremes, we can be faithful to uphold the charge of the Apostle Paul to "guard the flock," from false doctrine, manipulation and exploitation. God can use Pharisees, just like He can anyone who will be open to His loving direction and discipline. We see His theme of love running throughout the whole of both Old and New Testaments. He doesn't want our sacrifice, He wants our hearts.

In closing, I am reminded of the Broadway musical *Fiddler on the Roof*. It takes its name from one of Tevyah's opening lines. He relates that we are all like fiddlers, perched precariously on the roof of life trying to scratch out a melody. The musical powerfully drives home the tension between tradition and change. Tevyah and his family are caught between the old ways and changing values. We are caught in the same struggle but we have something that old Tevyah didn't have - the Holy Spirit.

NOTES

1.   Sam presented this paper at the Issachar Symposium at Aptos in 1994 and
      it is published in the upcoming book, ***Understanding the Times***, Straight
      Street Publications, 1994.

THE TASK OF FOURSQUARE MISSIONS AS IT RELATES TO THE CHURCH BOTH LOCALLY AND CORPORATELY

FRANK GREER

Purpose: The purpose of this paper is to: 1) examine current trends within the Foursquare Movement as pertains to foreign missions, 2) recognize the various entities that take part in missions, 3) formulate a strategy as to how they can mesh in order to accomplish the task and 4) provide a rationale for such a strategy.

CURRENT TRENDS AS I SEE THEM

There is a growing trend both within and without the Foursquare movement for what has been labeled **local church based missions**. The subject of the validity of sodalities[1] has been debated, discussed, passed off as being antiquated, and defended as being the only real way for missions. As a career missionary, I have only become aware of the magnitude of this debate since returning from Papua New Guinea where I spent ten years as a Foursquare Missionary. In January 1994, I accepted an appointment as the Asia Pacific Regional Coordinator for Foursquare Missions.

I observed what appeared to be an ever growing division between Foursquare Missions International, (hereafter known as FMI), and a number of key local U. S. church leaders. There were several issues that came to bear during this time. On the one side was a group of key leaders with churches that wanted to be involved in the great commission. This group appeared to have the opinion that much of what FMI was doing was not really relevant and that they, being successful in ministry here in North America, could be more effective in fulfilling the great commission if they bypassed the FMI program and went to other countries themselves. This, of course, fit with what some have called the Boomer Generation desire for relevancy, accountability, and involvement, which also would result in a sense of ownership, all of which are valid concerns. This also leads to the formation of a new sodality that fits with current trends.

On the other side was the established sodality, FMI, which viewed these leaders first with patronistic attitude, then with distrust, then with suspicion. As the division grew, FMI demonstrated defensiveness of what they knew to be the right way for missions to be done. The strategy being developed by the local church leaders, that of sending various kinds of teams to other countries and developing a relationship with one or more national churches, and making occasional visits to those countries was viewed by FMI as tourism in name of God, convenient missions, and something that would more than likely not have any lasting effect. Many times FMI was perceived as having a "You can't do that" attitude.

As I observed all this, it occurred to me that what needed to happen was that there should be a coming together, a partnering together of FMI with local churches to fulfill the great commission. I know there were others who were thinking this too. The Foursquare Missions Council was formed in May 1993 in response to this need. I also sensed that my purpose for being in FMI at this particular time was for the sake of working with and building relationship with the U.S. Church as much as it was for the sake of the Asia Pacific region. To this purpose I have committed myself.

WHAT IS NEEDED?

As I view the situation as it is currently, I believe the first thing that is needed is a paradigmatic shift on the part of both groups. This became convincingly clear to me as I came to understand that U.S. pastors felt that FMI viewed them as being inept when it comes to missions. The fact of the matter is that in some cases, (but not all), I did view some of the work that was being done by local pastors as being shortsighted and sometimes being of little or no effect. Why? Because of the paradigm in which these brothers were operating. The paradigm **assumes** (paradigms tend to do that) that aptitude (being adept as opposed to inept) is automatically transferable from one culture to another. However, successful ministry in one particular setting does not guarantee success in another setting, especially if that other setting is within another culture. When a person crosses that invisible line from one culture into another, everything changes. World view, ethics, a sense of good and evil, acceptable and unacceptable practices, habits, values, all of these things change. Consequently it is unwise, (arrogant?) for anyone to assume that they have the aptitude for something they have never done before, or done for a limited time. Immediate results can always be seen, but lasting results are the true indicators of fruitfulness. May I suggest that such a result as souls saved is not a trustworthy indicator of fruitfulness. In many countries around the world evangelists preach to people who have been "saved" several times before. A better indicator of fruitfulness would be a growing, healthy, reproducing community of believers.

Then there is the FMI paradigm, which I believe is changing, but had its own problems. We plagued ourselves with a patronistic, I-know-better-than-you attitude, that was quite evident to those local church leaders we dealt with. We demonstrated our attitude (arrogance?) in assuming that we always knew better than they did, and that our way, which had been tried and proven over decades of fruitful ministry, was the best. We prided ourselves that we did more with less and that we had honed our cross-cultural skills to a keen sharpness. Unfortunately, we honed our cross cultural skills so much in reaching outward to the nations of the world, we neglected to reach inward to our own constituency. We isolated ourselves from the U.S. church and thereby became, in their eyes, an unknown quantity, somewhat irrelevant to where they were as a church seeking to fulfill the great commission. We perceived any leader who was asking valid questions or trying something new as a threat to our program. So, we withdrew from these "thinkers" and left them on their own. Because of the way that Foursquare Ecclesiology works, FMI, which is dependent upon local churches for financial support, did not bite the hand that feeds it. But in many cases FMI simply turned loose of the hand that feeds it.

HOW DO WE CHANGE A PARADIGM?

May I suggest the use of Havelock's bridging strategy as a starting place. It consists of six interactive stages.

1. RELATIONSHIPS: The first thing that must be done is to bring the groups together in whatever settings are available and begin to talk about these things. FMI is currently making attempts to do just that. We are also exploring ways of involving local church people more in what FMI is doing. The key element to achieving this is communication.

    A. FMI must understand that local church leaders are hearing from God concerning missions. FMI must be willing to listen to what it is these leaders are sensing God is saying to them.

B.   Local leaders must understand that FMI does have experience in missions and can frequently help them discover what will work and what will not.

C.   FMI should abandon its "You can't do that" stance and listen first before making an assessment.

D.   Local leaders should abandon their "I'm going to do what God told me whether you like it or not" attitude and try to listen objectively to what FMI might say about a given situation.

E.   Both sides need to acknowledge that one cannot achieve maximum effectiveness without the help of the other.

F.   Both sides need to remember that a spirit of division and antagonism does not come from God.

2.   DIAGNOSIS: This should consist of three approaches:

    A.   Identify the Problems

    B.   Identify the Opportunities

    C.   Study the system as a whole in terms of what makes it up and what it is supposed to do to achieve some common goal.

3.   ACQUISITION: This has to do with resources which can be found through special people, group interview, observation, workshops. A key person in this stage would be a resource linker.

4.   CHOOSING THE SOLUTION: This can involve four steps.

    A.   Derive Implications from research.

    B.   Generate a range of solutions.

    C.   Test the feasibility of the recommended solutions through pilot programs.

    D.   Adapt the solution in order to make it fit the particular situation.

5.   ACCEPTANCE: This stage involves helping the participants to accept the innovation through a stepping stone process that does not overwhelm the participants.

6.   STABILIZING AND SELF RENEWAL: In many cases leaders will recognize that some programs have been put into place and are so embedded that it is impossible to bring outright change to them. This means there must be present the concept of ongoing renewal in order to bring about future changes.

I believe the two groups are communicating, and when both find out that other is not against them, then, when they pool their respective resources, they are in a position to form a strategy that has maximum effectiveness.

STRATEGIES, WHAT ARE THE OPTIONS?

Short Term Verses Long Term Missions

There are many opinions on both of these approaches, most of which seem to tout one as being superior to the other. I recently read in a short term missions teams paper the following answers to "Why do short term missions?".

1. It follows a biblical pattern
2. Participation of a great number of people
3. Cheaper and easier (As opposed to long-term missions)

The implication is clear. Short term missions, as opposed to long term missions, is more desirable, (better?). But to whom? Apparently to that great number of people who get to do it easier and cheaper and, oh yeah, we'll bless the nationals too. What I see as missing from that list of answers is something that speaks of its effectiveness. They seem to answer more of **what** it is than **why**. My point is this: First, most of us tend to assume that if one means is valid, then it invalidates or is superior to the other. And both of us can defend our position to the exclusion of the other. This is a serious error. How can I say that? Because I have come from a philosophical position, (long-term missions), that has told me that my way is right and superior. Then God comes along and stretches me in ways I could not have imagined and helped me to understand that there is validity in both of these methods of mission, and causes me to repent of my own arrogance in thinking that I had it all together. It is wrong for me to assume that because something is new and I have not done it, that it cannot work. It is also wrong for the other to assume that new is automatically superior to the older method simply because the new one is newer and the old one is older.

Second: It is wrong to assume that a new method should not be considered just because the old one is, in some people's minds, working just fine.

We must look at results. The old method has seen much in the way of good results. It has been found to be tried and true, therefore not something to be discarded. The new method shows great promise. It has not yet had time to develop a formidable track record. But I believe it will. So, do I believe in the concept of Short-term missions? YES I DO!! Do I believe in the concept of Long-term missions? YES I DO!!. Do I believe that these two methods can work effectively independent of each other? NO I DON'T!!

Why? First, because they need each other. The short-term missionary needs the long term-missionary to provide perspective, wisdom and experience that only time can provide. The long term missionary needs the short-term missionary to provide freshness, new perspectives, energy, vitality, and innovativeness that helps both the church and the missionary to continue to develop in ministry and fruitfulness. Second: because most national churches need both. During my time in PNG I saw that the national church needed me to be there for them all the time. But, they also needed the freshness of ministry that an incoming team could bring. There is the need for the infusion of the new and the continuance of the familiar.

A CASE FOR LONG TERM MISSIONS

How Long Does It Take?

In thinking of mission work, especially the work of attempting a church plant and hopefully the subsequent growth of a national church movement, the workers must think in the long term. Bringing the gospel into a culture that is unaccustomed to it, usually requires some dramatic change on the part of the recipients. This will inevitably take time, more time that we would usually predict. Hence a long term commitment is essential. Without this long term commitment, the results of the effort will be marginal at best.

What About a Long Term Commitment Using Short Term Teams?

I believe this to be a definite possibility. And I am supportive of people who would want to try it. There is a group of churches in the Northwest district who are making this attempt in Siberia. One of the problems that I believe they are currently facing is that they developed a plan in which they have overcommited themselves and are now experiencing a form of burnout. Hopefully they can get some more perspective on this, re-evaluate their plan, and then jump back in. Here is a place where they may need to consider the incorporation of a long term missionary into their strategy. As long as short-term teams are willing to make a commitment to the long haul, and not lose interest when the fascination and trendiness subsides, and when they have to deal with the everyday mundane issues of real life in a particular country, then I believe that they are a valid expression of a church walking in obedience to the great commission. This brings rise to a phenomenon that relates to this:

Centralized Missions Verses De-Centralized Missions

As much as we don't like it, there are some advantages to a centralized missions program. I occasionally interact with national leaders of other countries who have their own missions programs. I have been observing one in particular, to see how they will do, because they have in the last few years transitioned from a centralized to a de-centralized program. One major tendency I have observed is that they have tended to lose interest in some of the places they were previously committed to before they decentralized. Another tendency that I observed was that each local church began to attempt its own program. The result of this has been the lack of development of a country simply because church leaders lost interest, and what I call the "**Judges Syndrome**", each man doing what is right in his own eyes. In my opinion this church has lost some of its effectiveness as a missions church due to its decentralized program. We have had similar incidents in the U.S. church when local churches started their own missions program, and then when things did not go as planned, they bailed, (no other way to put it). Then FMI had to assume responsibility for the work. A centralized program provides a great advantage in terms of continuity and coordination.

When we think of New Testament missions we generally think of the apostle Paul, the book of Acts and the growth of the church. But, I would like to go back to the beginning of the Gospel and look at the foundation that was laid so that church could be birthed.

THE ESSENCE OF MISSION, INCARNATION

I believe the essence of mission is captured clearly by the apostle John in his writings. In John 1:14 he states, "And the Word became flesh and dwelt among us. And we beheld his glory, glory as of the only begotten of God. And He was full of grace and truth". This is the "going" of the great commission, when God left Heaven, went to earth, and lived with man. During this time the disciples lived with Jesus, walked with him, laughed with him, ate with him, saw him do all the miracles, heard all of his sermons, and learned what God is like. This is the challenge that we as God's servants face. People everywhere need to know what God is like. As we walk with God we can demonstrate what God is like. as a missionary spends an extended amount of time on a particular field modeling the life of Christ before a national leader, this will have a lasting impact that cannot be fathomed. During my last term as a missionary to Papua New Guinea, I had been grooming a national leader to take my place as the highlands region supervisor for the church there. His responsibilities would be the oversight of 350 churches, plus administrating certain church funds and bank accounts. Because of his being groomed for the position, he was privy to the bank accounts and what funds were available. One of the topics that continually came up was that of designated funds. We would see certain needs arise and he, seeing that there was money in account would ask me why I did not use it to take care of the need. I would explain that I could if I wanted to, (that was how they thought about it), but, that because I am accountable to God and the church leadership, I would not use that money except for what it was designated for. When it was time for me to leave, this brother said this to me. I have watched you the whole time you have been here, (uh oh) and I see that you have always been honest, even when you didn't have to. When it comes to the use of this money, I want to be like you. I understand that this is the kind of man God wants me to be. To what do I attribute this? This man observed my life on and off for almost ten years, being with me constantly the last three years I was there. I was able to contribute to him a godly value that could only occur over a period of time. During my studies at Fuller Theological Seminary, Dr. J. Robert Clinton told us that values are *caught, not taught.* The point here is that important issues in national church leadership development, such as character and integrity issues, are something that must be communicated and modeled over an extended period of time. I cannot provide a statistic, but I can provide an observation. The majority of countries where FMI encounters large scale problems in the development of a national church are those countries where there was limited exposure to long-term missionaries. I can safely say, from my own experience thus far in working in Asia, that those Asian countries who have had no long term missionaries are the ones that are experiencing the most difficulties in their development. Why is this the case? I believe that it is because they have not had the opportunity of being impacted by incarnational ministry, which comes in the form of a person. In his first epistle John states that he saw, he heard, and he handled what pertains to the Word of Life.

Who Can Do This?

This is the good part. Because this can open the door for a great number of people. I have included with this paper an appendix that deals with the issue of sending what I call unskilled people. I probably could have found a better word to describe what I mean by that, but when you read it and understand the circumstance under which I wrote it, perhaps you will be gracious to me. Because of space I will not go into any more detail other than to state that I believe with all my heart that there is nothing that can take the place of John 1:14 incarnational ministry. It is, in my opinion, the essence of mission. We must remember, the ministry is not primarily a "what" or a "how". It is a "who".

CONCLUSION

What are the possibilities that can arise out of a partnership between short-term and long term missions, between a local church and FMI? I believe they are endless in terms of potential of effectiveness. Why work together? First, Time. If we communicate and coordinate together we will not be duplicating work anywhere. This would enable us to develop a strategy that is much broader than just one place and everyone would be able to see where they fit into the big picture. Second, FMI can help a church save time by helping it avoid reinventing the wheel. We really do have some people who know a lot. No brag, just fact. Third, A local church can provide FMI with 1. Human resources. Yes we are looking for a few good men and women. Where do long term missionaries come from? Many come from short term teams. After they were called to **go**, they were called to **stay** when they got there. 2. Impetus and incentive to set and reach greater goals. Why does FMI need this? Because it has become evident to us the we have in many ways slipped into a maintenance mode. We need to be revitalized. 3. The means to incorporate the local church into the overall strategy for the Foursquare Church around the world.

ADDENDUM TO PARTICIPANTS

Let's make a deal. If you talk to me I'll listen. If I talk to you, you'll listen. Jesus will help us.

NOTES

1.   The term sodality was coined by Dr. Ralph Winter to denote a parachurch organization such as a missions board, YWAM, and Campus Crusade. It is different from a modality in that it is not a local church based ministry.

APPENDIX

A RATIONALE FOR SENDING UNSKILLED PEOPLE
TO THE MISSION FIELD

By Frank Greer

On January 4, 1994 I was awakened in the middle of the night. I would like to say that it was just because the Holy Spirit woke me, but the fact of the matter was that I was sick as a dog and was coughing my aching head off. So much for spirituality. I got up and went to the living room so as not to disturb my wife in her sleep. As I lay on the couch, I began to think about our program of uninvolvement of church people in missions. Yes we have teams that go out from various churches. But are we really helping our people to answer the Great Commission?

I began to think about what might really be considered important about missions. Is it imparting all our church growth and leadership expertise that will make a difference in the people on the mission field, or is it the impartation of the life of Jesus in every day real life situations?

I had recently returned from a trip to Asia during which I spent time in Nepal and Singapore. I met several national leaders while I was there as well. I also was able to participate in a meeting called the Foursquare Asian Youth Congress. During this time I watched people (both young and old), come together for a week of fellowship and meetings. As this meeting progressed I observed just how much benefit the people who attended received just from being with people from other cultures and countries. It was an absolutely marvelous time in which people were able to fellowship with and minister to each other. Out of the 200 plus people that were there, only a handful had any kind of cross cultural training. The rest were just people who love God and wanted to share that love with others.

It occurred to me as I lay coughing on the couch that perhaps we are not doing all that we could in spreading the Gospel of Jesus. Perhaps we should be finding more ways for our local churches to be involved in missions in a more personal way. My reason for thinking this is because there is something that happens, something that is communicated, something that is given from one person to another that comes just from Christians being together, that cannot be organized, orchestrated, or outlined in a formal situation, such as the ones we professionals always think should happen when we are around. It is true that we who have expertise should be given the proper venue to share that expertise with those who need it. But we should not under-estimate what the spirit of God can do when an untrained Christian layman comes together with people in mission field countries.

I think it would be good to define what is meant in this paper by the term, "Unskilled Person". This terminology is used to describe a layperson from a local church who has gone to another culture and is sharing the life of Jesus that he/she has with whomever he/she is working. It is not that they are unskilled, as it were, but rather that they have had no formal theological or missiological training. It must be said that training does not necessarily qualify a person for cross cultural ministry. It must also be said that the lack of training should not disqualify a person from cross cultural ministry.

I recently returned from a trip to Asia where I had the opportunity to meet two young ladies who are working with the Foursquare Church in Nepal. One is a secretary and the other is a certified high school teacher. To my knowledge, neither has had any formal theological training or cross cultural training. They are from churches who have sent them out to serve as short term missionaries. As I watched these two persons move among the people in Nepal, I witnessed much ministry taking place through both of them. They have a genuine love for the people and have shown it clearly to the people of Nepal. In my opinion they have done much to solidify in the hearts of the people of Nepal that Jesus is real and that following him leads to eternal life.

In turning to the Scripture I noted two interesting incidents. In Matthew 8 we see Jesus raising Simon Peter's mother-in-law from the dead. What was her ministry? To serve others. After being raised from the dead, she fixed dinner for Jesus and the disciples. In another incident, found in Acts 9, Peter raises Dorcas from the dead. She is called a disciple and she had gone around helping the sick and the poor. Why was she raised from the dead? So that she could continue the ministry that God had given to her. There is something about seeing Christianity lived out in the mundane things of everyday life. It touches people's heart right where they live.

I am reminded of a story that I heard about a missionary who served in Africa. He was not skilled in biblical training. He was just a mechanic. He kept all the mission vehicles running, as well as the stations generators. . He would also help the nationals with their motor bikes and bicycles. He did not teach in the Bible School or even preach in the churches there. For years this particular mission had worked among these people with limited results. One morning the mechanic, got up and made a fatal mistake by not shaking out his boots before putting them on. A scorpion had crawled into his boot during the night. He was stung by the scorpion and died. When the day of the funeral came, hundreds and hundreds of the local people came for the funeral. The missionaries were quite surprised, because up until that time, the locals had shown such little interest in them. After the funeral, the tribal leaders came to the missionaries and said we want to become Christians. We want to follow Christ. The missionaries were quite puzzled by that and asked them "Why?" They replied that the missionaries had been telling them about this God who loved them and had died for them. They told the missionaries that the only missionary that they had seen really live what they were preaching was the mechanic. And when he died, the people knew that he had given his life for their sakes, that he didn't have to come there and die, but that he had chosen, out of love for these people, to come and lay down his life on the mission field. His "real life witness" was stronger than all the other missionaries. The result of this missionary's life and subsequent death was that a revival began among the people.

I believe that there is room on the mission for both skilled and unskilled people to help in the cause of Christ. Working together they can have a double impact on a particular group of people.

Why should this be done at all?
1. It does a work in both of the people, the one who goes, and the one who receives.
2. It kindles interest in the supporting churches.
3. It provides a greater sense of ownership for the local churches that has heretofore not been available to them.
4. It provides a model for everyday Christianity, not just for Sunday or pastoral Christianity.

As we are told in our churches, everyone is called to go. We can help to provide a means to this if we are willing to do so. Remember that we are all called to go, but not all are called to stay once they get there. There will be those who are called to stay in certain places in order fulfill their destiny in God. These are the skilled ones, the ones who will stay long-term to teach, train, develop, and encourage leadership in the various countries. Is there room for both? Yes, In fact I would go so far to say that one is lacking without the other.

LEADERSHIP: DEFINING GREATNESS

John Honold

INTRODUCTION

I recently read an article in Time magazine which featured 50 of America's most promising leaders under the age of 40. While some names were recognizable, others were not. Every person had been photographed, and a brief description of their accomplishments listed. The group was touted as having the "requisite ambition, vision and community spirit to help guide us into the new Millennium."

Several things touched me as "significant" as I read the article.

Many of the featured leaders were from special interest groups or associated with groups that represented a "cause"; the writer was unclear as to what type of leader would be the leader of the next generation, as surmised by the variety of people featured as well as the accompanying article; and finally, that this group was my peer group, and no pastors were among them.

What would a list of America's most promising pastors under the age of 40 look like? What would be the appropriate criterion to make such a list?

Now the compiling of such a list is not the subject of this paper nor my personal desire. This paper addressees significance and greatness in terms of the Kingdom of God. My specific focus will be on what makes a great pastor, which ultimately leads to what makes a great church.

MEMORIES FROM THE FIRST MOON LANDING

July 20, 1994 marked the 25th anniversary of man's first walk on the moon. This great achievement had a profound impact on me as an eight-year old, and revealed a portion of my character that would later be a great source of conflict as a Christian.

Our family was in Hayward, California. My father, a US Marine, was about to be shipped out to participate in the Viet Nam War. The thoughts of war were very briefly held in check as Apollo 11 soared towards the moon. On the day of the landing, we all huddled in front of the television and watched, held our breath and waited. Upon touching down, we all collectively sighed and then celebrated!

Several hours later, Neil Armstrong and "Buzz" Aldrin became the first humans to ever walk on the moon. Amidst the fanfare and commentary of the various groups on TV, one voice interrupted, saying "Don't forget about me!" It was Michael Collins, the third member of the Apollo 11 crew. He didn't make it to the surface of the moon. His job was to stay in the spacecraft, circling the moon and making sure that everyone got back to earth.

I distinctly remember the feeling I had upon hearing Collins' voice. I thought, "Oh God, I never want to be left behind. I want to be first, I want to be the one who does the main thing". Thus began the adventure, the "quest to be the best".

WHAT DOES THE BIBLE SAY ABOUT GREATNESS?

The Bible shares in Mark 9:33-37 about a discussion the disciples had about the subject of greatness. The actual content of the discussion is unknown, but the conversation (argument actually) is asked about by Christ, bringing about a very uncomfortable moment.

> "They came to Capernaum. When He was in the house, he asked them, 'What were you arguing about on the road?' But they kept quiet because they had argued about who was the greatest." (33-34)

What brought this conversation about? Twelve men who were with the Lord everyday, the future leaders of Christianity, arguing about who is the greatest. Jesus asks for an answer, and they kept quiet. Why? Because they're embarrassed. This is not the kind of thing that grown men are supposed to do. But, Jesus brings it to the forefront by gathering them together and sitting them down. It's time to learn.

Reading this, I thought of times in my life where I have struggled with my flesh this way. Being "too" aware of other church sizes. Wanting to hear how the message went, again. Getting into friendly conversations with other pastors and walking away and playing comparison.

Jesus asked the question because He knows the hearts of men. He used the opportunity to address a common issue of the flesh and brought out it into a healthy perspective of the spirit.

> "Sitting down Jesus called the twelve. 'If anyone wants to be
> first, he must be the very last, and the servant of all.'" (35)

Jesus shares something totally opposite to what they have been exposed to. It is revolutionary, in that the leadership of the local synagogues, the ruling elders and even the Sanhedrin are leaders that lived a life of lordship and separation from the common people. In a poverty-stricken society, to think of being the very last is resigning oneself to being hungry.

However, we see in the life of Christ many incredible examples of servanthood, and thinking of others before himself. One situation that especially stands out to me is in John 13, where Jesus washes the feet of his disciples. In that great meal known as the Last Supper, none of the twelve had taken the initiative to offer hospitality and welcome each other (washing the feet of all those who enter). Jesus, being fully aware of who He was, where He had come from, and where He was going, simply took off His shirt and washed the feet of the twelve.

He continues in Mark 9:36-37:

> "He took a child and had him stand among them. Taking him
> in his arms, he said to them, ' Whoever welcomes one of these
> children in my name welcomes me; and whoever welcomes me
> does not welcome me but the one who sent me.'"

When adults walk up to my children, I watch to see the encounter. The first thing I notice is how they posture themselves. Bad posture is standing tall and talking down to a child. Good posture involves bending down and looking eye level with the child. It is a choice of making them look up at you or you coming down to them.

God loved us so much that He gave us his Son (Jn 3:16) who descended (Eph 4:9) to us, posturing himself so that He could see us eye to eye. God comes down to the level of his people. Pastors need to come down to the level of their people. We need to posture ourselves in a way that is non-threatening.

The second thing I notice is presentation. How does the adult talk to the child — does he grab for the child or extend his arms out in a safe way? How does the child respond to him? How do they respond to the reaction to the child? Children often wary of strangers and new encounters, tend to shrink back or remain silent. Adults are often offended by this.

Presenting ourselves to young children takes time. Easy language, a warm smile, and no great expectations. What ever they do is fine.

Our messages to the Body need to be easy to understand, in a language that is conducive to everyday life. They need time to reflect and digest the message, coming to a place where they can act in obedience. Our patience with new believers communicates hope. Grace. Unconditional love.

No where in this portion of Scripture do I see a rebuke for wanting to be great. As a matter of truth, the desire to be an overseer is a good thing (I Timothy 3:1). I do, however, see a radical re-defining of greatness that involved being last, serving all and welcoming children.

God says that the least in the Kingdom of Heaven is greater than John the Baptist (Matt 11:11). He promises that we will do even greater things in his name (Jn 14:12). What a secure place to be in when you can tell someone else that they'll end up doing greater things than yourself.

Why can Jesus say this? As mentioned earlier, Jesus is aware of who He is, where He came from, and where He is going (John 13:4). Pastors that understand their identity in Christ, have a proper perspective on their past, and a trust and confidence about their future (Call), can readily be last, readily serve, and readily welcome children.

In my first year of ministry (1984), two things happened that brought my desire to be first, to do the main thing, to a head. The first situation involved a trip in which three of our four staff would participate. I was told that I was to remain home. I was outraged! Immediately, I was Michael Collins, stuck orbiting the moon, while the rest of the staff got to play on the moon. My boss, sensing my vexation, told me that the very reason I was not going was that someone had to remain and care for the church. My angry reaction exposed an immature part of me that he addressed very quickly. He told me that I had to stop "wanting things," and understand what it meant to be faithful to a task, and obedient enough to carry it out with a sincere heart. I stayed home, but the issue was unresolved.

The second event happened two months later, when my boss removed me from leading worship. He explained that my worship centered on me and not Christ. I was "performing" and "flaunting" my ability just to be recognized. I was not allowed to play publicly for one year.

That year was painful, and the words of Jeremiah 45:5 became truth that I owned: "Do you desire great things for yourself? Do not seek them." Lesson learned. One year later, I was allowed to publicly lead worship. Six months after that, I became Worship Director, a position I would serve the Lord in for nine years.

My struggle came from drawing on how I felt about myself from everything I did, bending an ear to praise in order to feel loved and accepted by God. My struggle has been with the past, accepting the fact that I am dead to sin and alive in Christ. A proper perspective has allowed me to trust Him about the future. Pray for greater things to be done to and through the people around me. The results are awesome, and the beauty of what God sees as great motivates me to be last more, to serve more and to welcome the young Christians.

God has called us all to greatness in His sight. It is with a heart that is set on pleasing Him and not men (Gal 1:10). We are a church that the gates of hell will not prevail against (Matt 16:18). We have been chosen and appointed by God to bear fruit that will last (Jn 15:16).

GREATNESS AND THE CHURCH TODAY

In the time of Christ, the Jewish Leaders had sold-out to imagery and ornateness. They had segmented themselves away from the general community and subsequently communicated an unhealthy image of God to the people. The only image they were concerned about was how they looked on the outside. Jesus blasted this concern in Matthew 23. So warped was their view, that they debated what was greater, the Temple, or the gold of the Temple!

In this "age of the boomer" the church has grown up from it's hippie days in the '70's. During that time called the "Jesus Movement", Churches started emphasizing love, acceptance and forgiveness. The language of the church was easy to understand. Scores of people got saved, and many churches were planted. The folks who participated in this were primarily the group now known as the "Baby Boomers".

The "hippie churches" of the '70's became the established churches of the '90's. As "Boomers" matured, they brought into the church their ideas of excellence, of efficiency, "user-friendliness", the church as a "force" Vs a "fortress", "seeker services", church growth and church planting, re-emergence of lay leadership.

The hippies got richer. The church more established. The "Boomers" became good at church. And in this, there are some problems.

We've become very good at packaging our wares. There was a time that you could tell when "Church stuff" came in the mail. So we cleaned up our act. Now we look just like everyone else. That's OK, until we look at what folks are doing with all that mail that looks alike. The same thing that you do with it.

Now the proper response is not to "grunge" ourselves or revert back to the cut and paste days. The heart of what I'm saying is this: the younger generation is looking for something that communicates relationship — reality. And buying "signature software" and using plainer envelopes is not the answer.

Let's not lose the heart of Acts 2:42-47. Hanging out and solid relationships. We can keep everything else, but nothing beats a real face and real conversation.

Next in line are the folks of my generation (thirteenth, Baby Busters, Gen X, ?) As we are being positioned to take leadership, we are in a time of ascertaining how the church of the next millennium will look in light of the needs of the people around us. We cannot simply look at how our predecessors do church and imitate them. Ours is to understand why they did what they did and combine these whys with the what God had called us to specifically do.

Our generation (13th, X, Busters, ?) has been given the distinctive role of being the first generation ever to have a standard of living lower than our parents. Our generation is accused of lacking originality. Of settling for second or third best, because that's all we're going to get. The examples critics give are Woodstock '94 (an event produced by Boomers, attended by Busters, this time with corporate sponsors) and our inability to write an original music (in this age of "remakes").

Some of this may be true, but this is a generation that is hungering for relationship to the extent of settling for lesser jobs to spend more time at home. Marrying later in order to ensure that relationships last. And very intimidated by the success of the "Boomers" to the extent of behaving 180 degrees opposite. This desire for relationship, without the guidance of Biblical truth and a solid relationship with Christ, will result in selfish withdrawal. With Christ, it has the potential of being a solid gift of hope to the church.

What will the churches of the new Millennium resemble? Is there a way to adopt the energetic, strive for the best attitude of the "Boomers", with the strong relational and sacrificial attitude of the "Busters"? What will it take to produce "Great" leaders in the next ten years? The rest of this paper will deal with six elements of a "great" pastor.

SIX ELEMENTS OF A GREAT LEADER

1. A strong sense of "Calling"

In my first year at Hope Chapel Kapolei (hck), I experienced several set-backs that caused me to question my very existence in ministry. One week prior to our opening, I was kicked off of the local Christian radio station because of questionable remarks that I made. It devastated me, not so much to be off the radio, but for someone to question my ability just five days prior to the start of the church.

Of my first six staff selections, I had to fire two of them. While both decisions were right ones, I began to question my ability to pick and choose leaders.

Then there was the time I switched the collecting of the offering from the end of service to the beginning to allow for more ministry and worship at services end. Three weeks and $7000 in lost income convinced me that it wasn't wise at this time.

Right after I hired three full-time staff, attendance and tithe took a dramatic "nose-dive".

Amidst each of these trials, I questioned if I was the right person for he job. At each juncture, it was an assurance that God had called me into this new ministry that held me there. I have held to the promise of God.

Notice I did not say "vision". My former boss had a vision in which he saw himself lifted up in the air. My struggle is that I took his experience and made it an absolute for me. I waited for a "vision", that to this day, I've never had. At one point I even questioned if I was going out to pioneer because it was my boss' idea. It is the confirmation of call by God's Word that assures me that I'm right where He wants me.

"I have a Calling" should be an absolute at the heart of every pioneering pastor. It is a decision point in which a pastor can look back and be convinced about. A "Calling" is never borrowed. It is a Divine Appointment.

2. A Firm Hold Of The Word

Francis Schaeffer writes in his book, <u>The God Who Is There</u>, that prior to 1930, folks in the United States thought of life in two ways — right and wrong. There was a strong sense of morality, and if you violated it, you were quite aware of the choice you had made. After 1930, we saw in America the simplistic view colored by the emergence of compromising opinions, that later became socially acceptable alternatives.

Hebrews 4:12-13 states that the Word of God is living and active, and that nothing in all Creation is hidden from God's sight. That it can cut to the very source, separating bone and joints, soul and spirit. Paul told us of terrible times in the last days, and emphasized the importance of the Word as the way for the man of God to be thoroughly equipped (2 Tim 3:1,16,17).

The number of "causes" in our country are constantly on the rise. The emergence of "Global awareness" brings a multitude of issues, with a multitude of solutions proposed by everyone who has an opinion.

AIDS successfully became a moral issue when linked to Gay rights, (instead of a disease) and homosexuals are being treated like a minority race instead of people who abandoned natural relationships and were inflamed with lust for one another (Ro 1:26-27).

The Word of God must remain the relevant standard in an ever-changing world.

3. Grace

The absolute authority of the word includes the administering of the grace of God (Ro 3:23). The story of the Prodigal Son (Lk 15:11-32) is a beautiful example of the graceful heart of a father in light of a son who has lived a life of squandering the free gift the Father gave him. The older son represents the "veterans" of the body of Christ, who know what it is to be faithful and remain very steady, yet struggle with judgmental attitudes that make it virtually impossible for anyone to make a mistake and be received back into the Body.

Grace in the body of Christ is desperately needed between the older and younger brother combinations of the church. Older brothers need to develop a heart that forgives the squandering heart of the younger. And younger brothers need to learn what it is to be faithful from the older. It is this melding if generations that will insure greatness in the body of Christ for many generations.

4. Forcefulness

Matthew 11:11-12 describes those of the kingdom that forcefully lay hold of the things of God. It is a description of someone who is constantly grabbing, holding onto and acting on the things he is learning.

Forceful men and women are the response to a generation that is not reacting to the Gospel (Matt 11:16-19). The enemy has stepped up his assault on the human mind. This generation lives with every bit of information at it's fingertips. We are so assailed by violence and sex that we have become desensitized.

Active application of the Word "resensitizes" us. We are the salt and light of the earth. We cannot allow a fortress mentality to invade our thinking in light of the worsening situation in strategic cities and parts of our neighborhoods.

This has been a strong trait of the "Boomer" church. More than methods and "how to's", this Biblical precedent of "forcefulness" must be passed on. The next generation of pastors must stop letting their lives be dictated by the stock market, CNN, and incomplete news. The next generation of leaders must discipline themselves to constantly read, constantly research, and not give in to the television, media and magazines as the only source of relevant information. We need to keep in step with the Kingdom of God.

5. Prayer

I never considered participating in regular prayer meetings because I never saw myself as a potential "Prayer Warrior". Earlier this year I read Cindy Jacobs' book "Possessing the Gates of the Enemy". I realized that I have been short-changing myself, the church and the Lord by not stepping up my prayer life. As I developed the discipline of extended prayer time and re-acquainted myself with prayer lists, I saw marked differences in my life, especially this past summer, when I was praying a couple hours a night.

More than any other weapon we have in our arsenal, prayer is the quickest way to get the members of Body actively participating. It is the quickest way that the heart of God might be communicated to and through believers. And it is the quickest way that the power of God is realized.

6. Understanding "Whys" and Establishing Values

Does this new generation have any original ideas? Or are they destined to copy everything from someone else? Tom Peters wrote, in what has become a standard phrase of the '80's and '90's: "Form follows Function". This has been the rallying cry of companies re-organizing and constantly adjusting and adapting to an ever-changing market.

Focusing on "form" is either an exercise in self-preservation or in fear. Either way, the key to finding out is asking "why". This area is vital for the next generation. We are a society being taught: "why ask why?" and "Just do it!" It is an area where the teacher of values must be patient.

To a generation that is being conditioned in three to five minute attention spans (avg. length of TV scenario between commercials), the process could be painstakingly long. But this area must be mastered and constantly applied to every situation encountered. As I mentioned earlier, the discipline to not yield to the "easy road" is critical.

CONCLUSION: RELENTLESS PURSUIT TO BECOME CONTENDERS

I'm a Forty-Niners fan, from the days of John Brodie and Gene Washington to the current combination of Steve Young and Jerry Rice. But in the Jimmy Johnson years of the Dallas Cowboys, I must say I was impressed. In a span of four years, he took a 1-15 team to a Super Bowl victory. Four years at the helm and they were contenders.

What will it take for the next generation of Pastors to become contenders?

1. Understanding of our call to greatness as defined by Jesus Christ. It is a call to not worry about being first, to serve, and to keep it simple. In order to live up to this call, we need to have a proper understanding of our identity in Christ, and a Biblical perspective on our past and future.
2. "Call"
3. The Word
4. Grace
5. Forcefulness
6. Prayer
7. Whys and Values

That first moon landing revealed flawed thinking in my life. I needed to be the main guy, never left behind and I could not stand the thought of missing out on anything. In retrospect, I consider it a privilege to be the Michael Collins of our church — leading people to be their best, providing a return to safety in the Lord, and helping them answering their call to serve. The redemptive power of the Cross has helped me to see the flaw and know the truth, which now has set me free (Jn 8:32).

It is time to blend the best of previous Generations with the best of what the leadership of the Millennium have to offer. May they do greater things.

RECLAIMING MINISTRY TO
THE WOUNDED

Mark Hsi

I am troubled by the plethora of Christian counseling organizations that seem to be springing up like mushrooms all over the landscape. I listen to the radio and hear that I should send my troubled teen (if I had any kids, of course) thousands of miles away to an inpatient counseling clinic where he or she can find real hope for their problems. I see advertisements for Christian therapists that will mend my broken soul (and I can even use my insurance!). Counseling books galore can be found at any Christian bookstore as well as tapes, videos and even a Bible geared to people in recovery groups. What is going on? Are Christians so beat up and filled with traumas and troubles that they need all these services? How should we in pastoral leadership respond to this alarming phenomena? Should we cluck our tongues and speak out against this alternate religion, as David Hunt sees it? Do we need to invent new styles of ministry in the Christian community to accommodate a bunch of screwed up baby boomers and busters that are clogging up the normal avenues of care? Or do we need to look closely at what is going on in this counseling boom and pray to see the heart of God in caring for His people.

What would lead a Christian to seek emotional healing at a parachurch organization? Why would someone feel the need to be ministered to outside the confines of their local church? What does the presence of parachurch counseling ministries tell us about the perceived ability of the local church to heal its wounded? On the first day of classes at the seminary I attended, the director of my Marriage and Family Counseling program gave us a brief history of Christian counseling. He informed us that Christian counseling initially took its lead from secular theorists rather than from church sources. Arising out of the desperate need of the people of God, Christian counseling sought to address the brokenness that the church seemed impotent to heal. The obvious danger, he stated, was that Christian counseling lacked the theological integration to ensure Biblical soundness. While we were to learn secular theory and techniques to counsel the broken among God's people, we were encouraged to work out a Biblical theology to justify what we were doing.

It seemed that our existence as counselors was determined more by the need of God's people rather than a theological grasp of the ministry of Jesus Christ. Our handbook for healing was only secondarily the Bible and we learned to be more therapists than ministers. Yet, many Christians grew to rely on Christian counseling as the remedy to their woundedness. Rather than finding hope and healing in the local church and its ministries, believers looked outside to get their needs met. Christian counseling arose to meet a need that the local church was not filling. The obvious question is whether or not the local church was ever given the commission to mend the wounded and heal those who were sick in body and soul. If the answer is yes, then we must wrestle with why such a commission has been neglected and what must be done to correct such an omission.

The solution to our dilemma is really not as easy as most may seek to resolve it and perhaps not as difficult as others may feel. I will explain my enigmatic statement. The solution that many churches have adopted to address the counseling needs of its people is to offer Christian counseling as part of its services to the congregation. This is accomplished quite simply by hiring a staff counselor or two who have had a degree in therapy. These individuals may or may not have attended a Christian therapy program, but by virtue of their faith in Jesus Christ, qualify as 'Christian' therapists. I myself once interned at a church in California that had two full time therapists, one part time, and myself as a part time counseling intern. People seeking assistance were referred to us and we conveniently served to ease the counseling demands of the pastoral staff. The counseling ministry was a bit of a 'out of sight, out of mind' situation for the church leadership and we were not integrated into the main thrust of discipleship, evangelism, and teaching in the church.

The problem with this all too common solution to the counseling dilemma is that the needs of the people of God are not addressed in the context of the normal ministry of the church, but rather by a specialty ministry led by people whose primary credentials are secularly driven. I graduated from the Marriage and Family Counseling program of a well recognized seminary and can speak with authority when I say that even programs in Christian institutions are primarily secular in their education of people training for a career in counseling. In order to prepare its graduates to meet state and national regulations for licensed therapists, accredited programs must adhere to strict curriculum requirements. I do not blame Christian Counseling programs for being secularized; they need to exist within a world that demands validation for practicing professionals in the industry. Yet, does the church need more professionals to meet the needs of its people? As most clergy would agree, the seminary experiment has largely failed in its mission to prepare neophyte pastors to lead God's people. In the same fashion, counseling professionals trained in accredited institutions are not the answer.

At the risk of needless repetition, the problem is not with Christian counselors but with pastors. We speak of equipping the people of God for the work of the ministry and then tell them that some problems and some people are best dealt with by the professional, the Christian counselor. On the other end of the spectrum, we correctly affirm gifting and calling but neglect adequate training in the usage of such gifts. Having a rocket grenade launcher is not as good as having one and knowing how and when to use it. The scriptures speak of the weapons of righteousness that "have divine power to demolish strongholds" (2 Corinthians 10:4b). Perhaps every Christian needs just such equipping to accomplish the works of Christ to set people free from strongholds and their bondages to sin.

The problems that people bring to the counseling room are really not so unusual. That does not mean that they are not severe, only that the problems are similar to ones that have always existed since Adam and Eve disobeyed God. The work of the church has always been to do the works of Jesus: to preach the good news to the poor , to proclaim freedom for the prisoners, to recover the sight of the blind, and to release the oppressed (Luke 4: 18). God has made available to the church the fullness of His presence in the Holy Spirit, the Counselor that will convict the world in regard to sin and righteousness (John 16:8).

God has not left His church at its wit's end in trying to deal with the multitude of problems that modern man in all his dysfunctional glory brings to the table. I do not believe that God has risen up counseling ministries to solve the problem of a church that scratches its head wondering why the 'normal' ministries of preaching, Christian education, and cell groups do not make it for all the people. I do not think that God would have us progress with business as usual and ship off the weird and troubled ones to our evangelical leper colonies, the EGR (extra grace required) groups and the 12 Step (fill in the blank) programs. The main ministry of the church, the 'normal' programs, need to be effective for all the people and particularly those who are poor in spirit, who are in bondage both spiritually and emotionally, and who are oppressed. The church of Jesus, who said, "It is not the healthy who need a doctor, but the sick" (Luke 5:31), should do no less.

In Matthew 18, we are introduced to a question of significance. The disciples are in the middle of a conversation (Luke 9 calls it an argument) about what constitutes greatness in the Kingdom of God. They call upon Jesus to settle the question, with each presumably hoping to have some quality uniquely representative of them self held forth to be indicative of true greatness. Strength, courage, boldness, efficiency, tough mindedness. Instead, Jesus calls a little child to his side and says: "I tell you the truth, unless you change and become like little children, you will never enter the kingdom of heaven" (Matthew 18: 3). I would imagine that in Jesus' day, much like our day, that children had significance in the 'seen and not heard' classification of life. Adults so rarely take children seriously; in a world of bottom line results and decisive actions, children seem to just get in the way. Yet, contained in the miniature body of the child and in the naivete of a mind so unexperienced lies the key to not just greatness but entrance into the Kingdom of Heaven. The strong would need to take lessons from the weak, the knowledgeable from the inexperienced, and the significant from the insignificant. Perhaps this same lesson applies to our dilemma today. Perhaps the weakest in our midst, the one most oppressed, holds the keys to a type of ministry where the the poor in spirit can have their fill of the Kingdom of Heaven and those who mourn can find rich comfort in the arms of God.

Little children want to be understood. Not in a lofty, know it all way, but in a way that sees the world through their eyes. Even a small child can sense when they are being patronized, even if in a nice way. Compassionate ministry has the same starting point: to understand every hurting, broken down, and discounted person from their own perspective. To seek to understand their world, their experiences, their wounds through their own eyes and to see in the most lowly of them, ourselves. 'But for the grace of God go I' needs to be more than a statement; it needs to be the revelational grasp of our own sin nature that bonds us inexorably with the one we would least seek connection with. There really is not much difference in ministering to the strong as to the weak. We do wrongly when we invent two languages for the strong and the weak: the disciple and the dysfunctional, the anointing and the addiction, the equipper and the enabler. When you seek to understand what an adult is, it is beneficial to first look at a child. When you seek to understand what makes the strong, it is helpful to first look at what makes one weak.

When your child shows up at your doorstep a muddy mess and proceeds to give you a long winded and detailed description of not only how they got introduced to mr. mud hole but the absolute, inescapable logic of why they met him, they are telling you that you need to know how they came to be in their particular mess. But, when they hold up their arms to be picked up to be cleaned, they are saying "could you be big and strong and take care of me no matter how I came to be such a mess?" It is important when dealing with the hurting that you understand not only how they came to be such a mess but how to get them out of it. A listening ear and a sympathetic spirit is good but not enough to offer real assistance. If you brought your car to be fixed by a mechanic and he listening empathetically to your vehicular woes but did little else, you would leave understood but not helped.

"Come to me, all you who are weary and burdened, and I will give you rest" (Matthew 11:28). Jesus Christ offers to the over burdened real assistance, tangible assistance, assistance that makes a difference in the torment of a soul. So how did Jesus become so good at helping people? Unfair question, you might say, because Jesus had the full advantage of deity in knowing how to help people. Yes and no. Jesus had the fullness of divinity to back Him up, but I think He learned about helping people by first becoming a person. The scriptures report that "He did not need man's testimony about man, for He knew what was in a man" (John 2:25) up close and personal. I think Jesus learned about people as He grew as a little child into mature adulthood. He saw around Him, probably even within His own family, what made people hurt and troubled. Remember, that none of Jesus' family, outside of Mary, believed in Him and that His earthly father never saw Jesus' ministry. He saw within himself, the tension between sin and obedience, and knew first hand the twisted appeal that sin makes: "For we do not have a high priest who is unable to sympathize with our weaknesses, but we have one who has been tempted in every way, just as we are-yet was without sin" (Hebrews 4:15).

Ministry to the hurting begins with knowledge about people and what makes them broken and bent. Like Jesus' ministry, this knowledge needs to be first person: "a man of sorrows and acquainted with grief" (Isaiah 53:3b). What makes people so broken? The easy answer is sin. We have problems because we sin. If we would acknowledge our sin and repent of it, our lives would be mended.

"I agree, but, pray tell, which sin?"

"Why, the sin that brought you in here. You know, the sin of alcoholism."

"Okay. I confess that my alcoholism is a sin and I repent of it. Is that it?"

"That's it. You are free."

"But what do I do about my boss? You know that my boss reminds me of my father who I have always hated. Every time I get chewed out for something I don't think was really my fault, I get depressed and start drinking again. Sometimes I feel like I can't trust those who have power over me; I know that they will somehow use that power against me. I know it's wrong, but I sometimes I think that God is out to get me too. I know I'm no good and if it wasn't for Jesus, God would just let me have it. When I feel like my life is going out of control, I reach for the bottle-it smooths out my wrinkles and I can go on again."

Does this man have a problem with the sin of alcoholism? Of course, but possibly the drinking is just a symptom of larger and more concealed sins. Bitterness, unforgiveness, self hatred, distrust of God, fear that manifests as control, rebellious attitudes. People familiar with Alcoholics Anonymous will tell you that when people start sobering up, other addictions such as sexual immorality, eating disorders, and workaholism start to have a field day. Sometimes the sin that you can see is only the visible tip of an iceberg-like sin structure that freezes the person into his bondage to sin. Most every sin does not exist in isolation but in community, supported by other sins that accommodate and facilitate its existence. People sin because it works, if only for a season. Sin meets a need, a real, tangible need that in itself is not sin.

Our alcoholic friend has needs. He needs to know, in his heart and not just his head, that he is valued by a God who loves Him. He needs to know that he is not what others say He is but who God says he is. He needs to know that God's mercy and grace forgives his sins and empowers him to forgive those who have hurt him. He needs to know God as a Father, not just know about Him as a deity. In the absence of God's real care, this man can only turn to his sins. His self hatred validates the hard existence he leads and makes sense of the hatred he has felt his whole life. His resentment towards his boss and father meet his needs for justice against those who hurt him and against whom he feels powerless. His alcoholism is a response to his need to feel a bit of comfort that he, and no one else, can control. His distrust of God is his way to somehow protect himself from one bigger and stronger than himself.

Yes, he needs to repent. But be careful that a band aid solution not take the place of a surgical repair of the heart. A wise physician will ask questions like the following when making a diagnosis: "when did you start feeling this pain? Did it increase or decrease when you walked? Any history in your family? Are you under abnormal stress?" He does so because diagnosis is critical in treatment. And diagnosis is based not only on a complete history of the condition but an understanding of the logic of the condition, the whys as well as the hows of the condition. When you walk through the lives of the broken, you will find that their brokenness makes sense given the circumstances that surround, precede, and give birth to such brokenness and sin. When destroying strongholds, it is helpful to have the original floor plans so that you can selectively demolish the structure's main supports. Certain sins, like unforgiveness, rebellion, and blasphemous notions of God, have a way of clogging up the flow of God's grace in bringing wholeness in Christ: "See to it that no one misses the grace of God and that no bitter root grows up to cause trouble and defile many" (Hebrews 12:15). Sin has its own perverted logic and appeal and the process of repentence often times requires the destruction of "arguments and every pretension that sets itself up against the knowledge of God" (2 Corinthians 10:5). Recognizing the basis of the sin strongholds helps to expose its depraved wisdom and bring it to obedience to Jesus Christ.

Does understanding the rationality for sin give license to sin? Do broken people adopt a victim mentality that shirks personal responsibility for sin? Does a person with a broken limb claim the right to be lame because he understands the physiology of his shattered bone? Or does it not make him more careful to avoid such situations after he gets healed? People who do not want to take personal responsibility for their sin do not truly want to get healed. As Jesus asked the man by the pool of Bethesda: "Do you want to be healed?" (John 5:6). He would not heal one who really wanted no healing.

And what is this man healed by? He is healed by the love of God. "The Lord is close to the brokenhearted and saves those who are crushed in spirit" (Psalm 34:18). The love of God affirms man's greatest need: "What a man desires is unfailing love" (Proverbs 19:22). Repentance then, is not so much the actions of one escaping the wrath of God but the response of one who is truly loved: "God's kindness leads you toward repentance" (Romans 2:4). The revelational experience of God's love is the way out of the bondages of sin. Although sin works to meet a need, obedience works much better. Like Saul on the road to Damascus, we become ambushed by the love of God. Saul's road to Damascus became his road to repentance, God's invitation to grab hold of life. People are led from their places of brokenness when they have "power, together with all the saints, to grasp how wide and long and high and deep is the love of Christ, and to know this love that surpasses knowledge" (Ephesians 3:18-19). Love truly covers over a multitude of sins.

How do we accomplish all these things? Am I saying that we need to spend voluminous hours counseling our people into wholeness? Last I checked, there is no reference to counseling as a specific gift of the Holy Spirit. The Holy Spirit, however, is called the Counselor who will convict the world in regard to sin and righteousness and guide believers into all truth. The Holy Spirit is at work in the lives of Christians to mend and to heal, to expose the sin structures behind visible, symptomatic sins, and to lead the broken into the healing presence of Jesus Christ. Our job as ministers is to learn to work with the Holy Spirit, to facilitate an atmosphere in personal and corporate ministry where the Holy Spirit can convict of sin and lead to righteousness. The minister becomes an interpreter of the ministry of the Holy Spirit for the congregation. As we Christians learn to become sensitive to the movement of the Spirit in our lives, we learn to cooperate with and not quench the Spirit. The work of transformation is bore by God's Spirit and we become the facilitators of this transforming work in corporate worship, preaching, cell group ministry, and personal times with Jesus. Ministry in the Spirit takes on a new meaning as we learn not to perfect in the flesh what was started in the Spirit.

All too often, Christian counseling becomes reduced to just such a striving in the flesh for what God would accomplish through His Spirit. We can spend countless hours speaking truth and searching out issues that seem to fall upon deaf ears. The Holy Spirit is a much better counselor than you and I and able to bring revelational knowledge that strikes to the heart of the matter. I have seen the Holy Spirit speak countless times to broken people, showing them the sin structures that lay at the root of their problems. I have seen the Holy Spirit convict people of sins that they never knew they struggled with and repent of them with tears of sorrow. I have seen people baptized with the Spirit of God as they repented of the sins God revealed to them. I have learned to be a better counselor as I learned to stop counseling and start facilitating in prayer that seeks the destruction of demonic strongholds with the revelational truth of God's Spirit. The issue at hand is not Christian therapy but Christian ministry that acts as the hands and heart of Jesus to lead His people from the brokenness of sin and into wholeness. I have yet to pray for a troubled person who has not contributed to their condition through their own sinful responses to often times brutal abuse. Yes, people have been victimized, but this fact does not exempt them from their responsibility to seek God's wholeness through repentance and obedience to His Word. We do not need to train skilled counselors but skilled ministers who can lead people into the restoration that comes at the hands of Jesus Christ. Ministry to the broken then becomes discipleship; a discipleship of the mended heart to Jesus and not just an outward conformity to a Christian lifestyle.

I read with great attention the words of God to the shepherds in the book of Ezekiel: "You have not strengthened the weak or healed the sick or bound up the injured. You have not brought back the strays or searched for the lost. You have ruled them harshly and brutally" (Ezekiel 34:4). I do not have right answers to some of the questions and issues I have raised. Hopefully, at least some of the questions have been on track to steer us to grapple with the church's ministry and the church's attitude towards those who are broken. Our Father cares for those who hurt: can we care for them also? Not just that we have feelings of care, but that we are fully equipped to care. Perhaps the answer is really not so difficult. Perhaps what is needed is less a "Seven Habits of Highly Effective Counselors" handbook and more a minister who knows what it is to be broken and weak before God. A minister who knows intimately the struggles of his own heart towards sin, the hidden sins of the heart like pride, control, rebellion, and insecurity. A minister who finds the comfort of God in the midst of sorrows and the humility of repentence for sins and the character structures that sustain such sins. A minister who knows that true strength is found in weakness that allows for the strength of the grace of God to shine through. The scriptures say that Jesus went outside the city gate to make us holy, making himself a virtual outcast to reach those who were themselves outcast. "Let us, then, go to him outside the camp" (Hebrews 13:13) to learn ministry that will heal a wounded world.

UNDERSTANDING WHY THEY DIED

Gary Matsdorf

"It's easier to birth a baby than raise a dead man" (Don McGregor). While interning at a church in Los Angeles where Don was an elder, I used to hear him say this time and time again. His immediate reference was to the relative ease of pioneering a church vs. trying to ignite a traditional/dead one. Thirteen years of pastoral ministry in Medford, Oregon have given me a deeper appreciation for Don's statement; only it's not with reference to churches/programs. The "dead" with whom I live are "mature" believers who, amidst an active, alive and growing congregation, have decided to leave the race of Christian service and church commitment for the good life on the back row.

We have had dozens of them; at one point, four former assistant pastors from other churches in Medford were attending FBC; at another point, seven of the founding elders of the largest church in the valley were attending — all vying for the back row! (In 1988, the Pharisee in me wanted to change our name to, "The Church of the Perpetual Dead". God said no.) Never being anything but 100% committed to the work of the Lord for some 26 years now, I struggled greatly with these deadbeats, praying constantly that God would send new people. And He did — of like kind.

About eighteen months ago, I began to wonder if perhaps God was trying to tell *me* something through these people. Had *He* sent them for a purpose that I had not yet understood? Did He want to use me and the ministry of FBC to lead them out of their current state into a fruitful future, or was each **a thorn...given me in the flesh, a messenger of Satan to torment me?** It took me nearly nine months to discover His answer — and it was not the latter.

The answer began with a prophetic word given by a reputable lady in the congregation during a Wednesday night service. The upshot of the word was that FBC was in bondage to fear — especially fear of intimacy with God and His work because of previously traumatic experiences in the lives of many of FBC's people; rather than being healed, these former "front runners" had quietly but firmly made decisions to never get hurt, burned out or "used" again. Solution? Go from the front row to the back, from being a front runner to a Sunday morning attendee. The only problem is — they unconsciously went to the back row with God as well. They developed subtle, almost undetectable, reserve toward God, lest His light shine too brightly in their hearts and show them their error.

I did not know what to make of the prophetic word when it was delivered. "Fear of intimacy with God?" I thought. "Give me a break. They're <u>willful</u> Moabites who just need to get off their duffs, **be serious and discipline [themselves]** (I Peter 4:7). After all, **'No one who puts a hand to the plow and looks back is fit for the kingdom of God'** (Luke 9:62)." Fortunately, rather than saying I did not see the word as applying to FBC, I had the maturity to say I would need some time to process the word before saying yeah or nay (cf. I Corinthians 14:29). My intent was to have it weighed by the eldership, whom I knew would confirm that FBC has its share of problems, but this is not one of them.

Was I wrong. After a time of prayerful deliberation, all but one elder agreed the word was God's very accurate diagnosis of where we were struggling. And how did they know? *It described each of them* — only they were hiding it with cosmetic serving. I was stunned; realizing that your discernment barometer is on Mars while your people are on Venus is not exactly ego inflating for any leader. That realization set off a three month search for understanding, followed by an eight week preaching series on fear at FBC. Before I share why I have chosen this topic for this paper, let me share some of what I discovered in my study about fear.[1]

1. Fear is both a psychological and spiritual problem and much of life is spent negotiating the maze of fear. Fear anticipates punishment and often makes real the pain it imagines (I John 4:18).

2. Fear is usually neurotic and driving; it causes us to resist truth (John 8:32; Hebrews 2:15).

3. Fear is usually our first response to a sense of failing God; it misreads His nature (Genesis 3:10; Exodus 34:6-7).

4. God's endeavor to guide us out of fear often mysteriously backfires, causing us to want to run all the more or at least to skirt the real issues (Genesis 3:11-13; Romans 7:7-25).

5. Fear thrives by assuming the dread of the past will resurface in the future.

6. Fear results from misreading life (Mark 4:35-41; James 1:2-8).

7. Fear easily camouflages itself.

Mike Yaconelli is right —

Fear is a mysterious visitor — an uninvited guest. Fear is elusive and threatening. It is difficult to identify and harder still to admit. Once it visits, fear tries to move in permanently, and hold us hostage — cancelling out our reason, our faith, our dreams.[2]

This was the people of FBC and I was afraid to admit it; I was not wanting to admit their lack of committed service could be the result of anything but willful stubbornness. Furthermore, rather than wanting to see them change, I was wanting to see God fry them; like Jerry Falwell or Rush Limbaugh with President and Mr. Clinton, I would have rather shot them than pray for them. After all, they were impeding the church's progress; leeching rather than giving; withholding much needed money and service; creating additional work and stress for me; I, Pastor Gary E. Matsdorf, who has **been very zealous for the Lord...I [who] alone am left** to work while they watch, was not about to cut them slack. Then God spoke...through a woman (why hadn't I listened to Paul's command that **in all the churches of the saints, women should be silent in the churches?**); He then confirmed by the elders (why did I install them anyway?).

What does all this have to do with being an Issacharite? I think plenty, for not only have I emerged from this five month experience feeling like a "born again pastor", but I feel like I have made some key observations that are applicable beyond the borders of FBC (which, by the way, is radically changed as a result of these recent events).

1. **Double-minded saints.** James 1:7-8 has always intrigued me — **for the doubter, being double-minded and unstable in every way, must not expect to receive anything from the Lord.**[3] Who does not doubt? Why would God link it to being **un-stable in every way**? It cleared up for me when I discovered that **double-minded** translates *aner dipsuchos* (literally, a "double-souled" person). It means on one hand to trust God, yet on the other hand to have reservations toward Him <u>because</u> of an inadequate understanding of life's experiences and His place in them (James 1:2-4). It describes the saints in Hebrews who are misreading their experiences (12:3-11) and are hence perilously close to **fail[ing] to obtain the grace of God** (12:15A). They are **unstable in every way** because they are not quite sure what to make of God as a Person — and if they are unsure about His personhood, it is down hill from there. This leads to the possibility of **a root of bitterness** springing up and causing trouble and defilement (Hebrews 12:15B). And what is this **root of bitterness**? In its most extreme form it is outright rebellion against God (cf. Hebrews 12:16-17). But for most Christians, the

bitterness is a subtle reserve to commit to God (Luke 9:57-62), a reserve that eventually becomes defensive and rationalizes (cf. Deuteronomy 29:16-19).

I believe **double-minded** describes a lot of our people in a lot of our churches — and they need us to help them diagnose the root cause of their struggle, rather than attack their negative fruit.

2. **Victim mentality.** We live in a society in which it is "in" to claim victimization[4] and I fear this mentality has hit the pulpit. I fear as pastors/leaders, we all too easily process the difficulties of ministry through an "I" vs. "them" martyr complex that blurs the picture and prevents the real work of the kingdom from coming to fruition. "The victim...expects others to change or solve his problems and when they don't, he accuses and blames them for his plight."[5]

As pastors/leaders, we need to be quicker to admit that some of us are probably neurotic in terms of our susceptibility to feeling victimized by the people. What I was convinced were willful Moabites out to frustrate me were in fact double-minded people who needed a shepherd healthier than they to lead them to wholeness — not one wasting energy on dead-end emotional roller coasters of self-pity. (I believe those with a prophetic gift as part of their spiritual gift mix are particularly susceptible in this vein [cf. Elijah in I Kings 19].)

3. **We are the problem.** If God's chief purpose is to **present everyone mature in Christ** (Colossians 1:28), and if that comes about primarily through enduring trials (Hebrews 12:7), then it seems to me that *much* of the "tribulation" encountered in leader-ship is God's instrument for our perfection. (I say *much* because I do not want to forget the role of the devil, nor overlook the messes *we* create through immature, carnal behavior and decisions.) Is this not what God had to do with Israel following her deliverance from Egypt? Knowing that it is one thing to get God's people out of Egypt and quite another to get Egypt out of God's people, He tells Moses that they are going on a longer route back to Israel — all for the purpose of being taught a few things necessary to successful living in the Promised Land (Exodus 13:17-18A). He then embarks them on a 50 day journey to Mt. Sinai, stopping them seven strategic times to teach them seven vital lessons (Exodus 12- 17). (**Succoth** — learning that God is to be first in life; **Etham** — learning to submit to divine sovereignty and guidance; **Pi-hahiroth** — learning to live by faith and learning to live for God's glory; **Marah** — learning to deal with life's bitter experiences; **Elim** — learning to partake of God's abundant blessings; **the wilderness of Sin** — learning to partake of the life of God everyday; **Rephidim** — learning to wage spiritual warfare.)

And what is their response to all this? After untold times of neurotic complaining and rebellion along the way, they sell their souls for the cheap thrill of a drunken orgy (Exodus 32) — stretching the reasonably short trek from Egypt to Israel via Mt. Sinai into a 40 year circuitous trek in which their bones rot in the Sinai wilderness.

When I went to pastor in Medford in October, '81, I had no idea how immature and carnal I was in character, in spite of having had six years of "successful" ministry and two degrees in Bible. (There were times when I was so carnal you could have packaged me and sold me for 2 cents a pound at the local *carniceria*.) God kept orchestrating situations to perfect me, and I kept complaining."**Was it because there were no graves in [LA] that You have taken [me] away to die in [Medford]? What have You done to [me], bringing [me] out of [LA]? Is this not the very thing [I] told You in [LA], 'Let [me] alone and let [me] serve [in LA]'? For it would have been better for [me] to serve [in LA] than to die in [Medford]"**. (So what if I had spent two years begging God to get me out of LIFE and get me a pulpit?; we are talking emotional reaction, not reality.)

And guess what? I was not alone in my perspective or reaction. Rather it was an International Convention or District Conference, I found many others going through the fires of ministry who were not processing it any better than I. After we shared attendance figures (which were actually those of the last three Easters combined), I would listen to them complain about the negative people/things in their ministries, without one mention that perhaps this was God's "Hebrews 12" doing for their own sake. Somehow I feel He is often trapping those of us in vocational ministry against the backdrop of our own flesh, and we are either hitting rocks, binding the devil or giving Brother Smith the last fragment of our puny brains. And we wonder why He has to keep circling us back to Pi-hahiroth? Right!

4. **The importance of the prophetic Word**. The Baptist in me likes to believe that I am speaking prophetically every time I preach; the cautious pastor in me likes to keep the house rules for prophesying clearly focused before the people every Sunday morning; the Pentecostal in me wonders if the prophetic is operating enough at FBC; and the mercy of God is covering my backside — prophetically. I shudder to think where FBC would be today as a congregation were it not for the prophetic word on fear that came in September, '93. My challenge to all of us is that we will **...strive for the spiritual gifts, and especially that [we] may prophesy** (I Corinthians 14:1). I am particularly calling for striving for "diagnostic" prophetic words that discern the hidden realities going on in the life of our congregations; not that our customary, "I like you today

and am thrilled with your song list...thus saith the Lord", does not have merit; it is just limited.

But it is not just those who have "died" inside our churches who can benefit; I believe that understanding people's fears in the '90s and understanding the four observations I have concluded above will also increase our effectiveness in reaching our society. We as leaders desperately need to be as sharp and others' focused as we can be (cf. Philippians 2:4); we desperately need the Spirit to insightfully navigate us into their lives; they desperately need healthy and mature Church leadership models to counter the rebellion, disillusionment, self-focus and uncertainty they face everyday. They need us to be like David who **served the purposes of God in his own generation** (Acts 13:36).

Rebellion, disillusionment, self-focus and uncertainty. How did I come to those four conclusions? By looking at key American events in the '60s, '70s, '80s and first part of the '90s, surmising we are currently the sociological product of at least the last three and one-half decades. The '60s — a decade not only of Mickey Mantle, The Beatles, Andy Griffith and 400 HP ghetto gliders from Detroit, but a Decade of Rebellion. A decade in which our Supreme Court says an official "No" to God by banning prayer in public schools (June 25, 1962); a decade in which 55,000 young people storm the Pentagon in protest against Vietnam (October 21, 1967); a decade climaxed by 400,000 youth spending 60 hours in a rain soaked field in upstate New York — guzzling, snorting, shooting up, dancing and fornicating themselves into oblivion (August, 1969). Moving into the '70s, we encounter not only OJ Simpson, The Carpenters, streaking, Pet Rocks, Archie Bunker and Star Wars, but disillusionment, as Viet vets return to taunting crowds, a President and Vice-President resign amidst scandal, OPEC cuts our oil and our born-again President Carter is endlessly haunted by Murphy's Law; even heretofore inconsequential Iran, having captured 53 Americans, rises up to say, "Take that, you Western whoremongers".

Where to now? Maybe Hollywood can save us — and it seemingly does, as our actor turned politician President ushers in the glitzy '80s with new hope — complete with Nancy's $25,000. inaugural ball gown and subsequent purchase of a $209,000. China set for "quiet dinners and late night snacks". Nobody is going to keep Americans down! We come back fighting and fiercely independent, with Rambo as our hero; our no-nonsense Administration gives striking air traffic controllers pink slips in a move that signals, "Things are going to be different".

But all that glitters is not gold to the core. Not only does the Challenger explode, but so does the "Me, myself and I" movement. Self becomes king — two parent families hit an all time low of 27% as people bail from marriages in droves; Donald Trump buys half of NY city and names it after himself; even Jimmy goes from pounding pulpits to pounding doors with red porch lights.

And now it is the '90s — with life whizzing by at 90 MPH, 90 hour work weeks, 90 calorie diets because we are 90 pounds overweight and $90. minimum payments on our maxed out Visa cards — just to cover the interest. We are more cautious now — uncertain to be exact. Our goal seems to be little more than to be found alive, clothed and in our right minds by the year 2000. In 1816, Thomas Jefferson wrote, "I like the dreams of the future better than the history of the past". Americans in the '90s would probably not agree.

This being the case, we, as God's leaders, have to be the sharpest we have ever been; we have to be a step ahead — not licking our wounds and shooting at those we are called to lead. We have to hear the Spirit's diagnostic voice in and out of the Church and we desperately have to reach out to meet people at their points of fear. They have "questions of the uncertainty of the future, the crises of the present life and the unknowns of the past" (Hiebert). I only hope I am up and running enough to help them through all this. I only hope I have learned some key lessons — for the last time. They truly need someone who understands why they died — and are dying — may we the leaders in His Church be their faithful guides.

NOTES

1. All of these remarks about fear refer to harmful dread or terror. They do not apply to "healthy fear" — a proper respect or reverence for other people (cf. Leviticus 19:3) and especially for God (Proverbs 1:7).

2. Yaconelli, Mike, *The Door*, May/June, 1994, pg. 36.

3. All Scriptures, unless otherwise noted, are from the New Revised Standard Version.

4. It's too bad this concept has gone overboard, causing people to skirt personal responsibility and accountability, for many were legitimately victimized as kids and are yet suffering from it.

5. Cook, Jerry, "Healing Deadly Attitudes" in *A Reader on Healing & Wholeness*, 1994, ICFG Publications, Los Angeles, pg. 200.

JESUS THE DISCIPLE MAKER

Jeff McKay

Introduction

Christ's objective was to bring the gospel to the entire known world through his disciples. Considering the importance of this task it seems that some formal and organized approach would have been in order. Instead, Jesus choose ordinary men, trained them informally, and in three short years sent them as his representatives and missionaries. Christ's approach to discipleship was profoundly simple. He focused on the character development of his disciples. He didn't underscore many specific methodologies for ministry, but rather he transferred his values, and principles. Rather than communicating just knowledge he communicated life; his life.

There are six significant aspects of Christ's ministry to be considered:

1. How men came to follow him.
2. How Jesus ministered to those in pain.
3. How Jesus trained men for the ministry.
4. His priority of prayer.
5. His strategy for ministry.
6. His motive in ministry.

How People Came To Follow Jesus

When we examine the special dynamics involved in the disciples' call to become followers of Christ, we can draw four insights about evangelism and discipleship which may serve as underlying principles for our ministries.

First, we must recognize that coming to Christ involves a process. For example we can briefly examine the experience of Matthew, Peter, and Paul.

When Jesus called Matthew it was not the first time he had heard of Jesus' ministry. Jesus had set Israel astir with his message and miracles. Everyone was talking about the Miracle Worker and his radical message of freedom. All over Israel people were flocking to hear him speak with authority. He taught in parables, interesting stories designed to make truth understandable to those who would listen. All this intrigued Matthew. Imagine him sitting alone in the crowd listening to Jesus' words. How the Master's message touched his heart and gave him hope. How he wanted to also be a follower; but could it ever be? Later, to Matthew's surprise Jesus approached him and said, "Follow me." At this Matthew rose and followed.

Peter is introduced to Jesus some time before the miracle of the fish in Galilee, which seemed to have been a turning point for the disciples. Before that time they were with Jesus' ministry on a part time basis; but the time to leave all and follow Christ was approaching. Peter was cleaning his nets alongside the Sea of Galilee after a very poor day of fishing. Jesus was in the area ministering and asked Peter for the use of his boat to sit on and address the crowds. Later Jesus told Peter to push out for another catch. Peter reluctantly obeyed and that day he and his partners took in their biggest catch of all. It was obviously a miracle and affected Peter profoundly. Peter said to Jesus, "Go away from me, Lord, for I am a sinful man!" Jesus responded, "Don't be afraid, from now on you will catch men." Peter's feelings of unworthiness came from a guilty conscience. He had been resistant to a full time commitment to Christ because fishing was too important to him. However in the very area of his disobedience Christ pours out his grace upon Peter. In the moment of this miracle Peter's heart broke and he surrendered to Christ.

When Paul was converted on the road to Damascus Jesus said to him in a vision, "it's hard to kick against the goads". A goad was a sharp stick used to prod on a stubborn animal. The phrase in the text suggests the idea that Paul had been wrestling with conviction in his heart. God had been prodding Paul, but he had been resisting.

Second, we notice that people came to Christ through others. Most of Jesus disciples were introduced to him through another friend or family member. Andrew and Philip were introduced to Jesus by Jesus' cousin, John the Baptist. Later, Andrew found Peter his brother. They, later introduced their fishing partners James and John who were brothers. Other family relations can be found in Jesus' circle, for example Mary, Martha, and Lazarus their brother. Nathanael met Jesus through his friend Philip. There is even some evidence that Matthew's brother was James the son of Alphaeus another disciple of Jesus (Mark 2:13).

Effective evangelism and strong discipleship occurs in the context of families or strong friendships. This is because families and friendships are environments of trust, and trust is required in order for people to change. Methods of evangelism which introduce perfect strangers to the gospel may result in some fruit, but how much more effective would we be in recognizing that people change more readily in an environment of trust. Evangelistic events have value, but they are enhanced if a friend or family member brings the new person to the event.

Third, the Holy Spirit is the true agent of change in this process. God was working in the hearts of men to bring about surrender, which signals to us that salvation is a work of the Holy Spirit not to be rushed, but to be cultivated. We must be careful not to be "pushy" with the gospel in our evangelistic attempts, repelling people rather then drawing them. This summer while in Japan I made a friend, who later this year came with his wife for a visit. During his visit we had time to talk, a friendship was building, and a degree of trust was building. That Sunday, they came to visit our church and he responded to the salvation message. Another example is my father. For years I intentionally refrained from directly discussing the gospel with him. Only on rare occasions did we ever speak about this matter. Rather I concentrated on showing him God's love. Last year, immediately after his heart surgery in the hospital bed, he accepted Christ as savior. People come to Christ by the Spirit's power. We don't need to manipulate, force, or pressure people. Rather we are to build a trusting relationship with the person, and trust the Holy Spirit to draw them.

Fourth, in recognizing that people come to Christ primarily through a friend or family member, we can take advantage of this natural relationship they have with the one who originally brought them to Christ. This process offers a natural system of accountability in which follow-up and spiritual growth are reassured for the individual. We often create artificial systems that place new Christians with strangers to be taught the Christian faith. No one is naturally comfortable with that approach. Rather, in the context of a healthy church family the seeker or new Christian becomes involved with a group of believers he has met through his friend who brought him. It's this group of new Christian friends who begin to teach by example, deed, and occasional admonishments. They become the source of answers to his questions and give him a glimpse of how he is to live his new found life. This makes real change in the person's life more palatable since it's the influence of friends who love and care for the person.

Evangelism and discipleship must be simple, natural, and practical. These principles remove the pressure to have a complicated program which feels uncomfortable and artificial. Programs or methods still have their place, but only to compliment this process of human relations that God has already created.

How Jesus Ministered To Those In Pain

Jesus ministered directly to the place of spiritual need. He went past symptomatic problems directly to the root issue. Many of the surface problems people have are caused by lies they are believing, unforgiveness they are holding, feelings of guilt, rebellion, and the bondage of evil forces. His "tools" of ministry were truth, grace, forgiveness, surrender, repentance, and power over evil spirits. In Isaiah 61:1 we have a summation of Jesus' ministry style, "The Spirit of the Lord is on me , because he has anointed me to preach good news to the poor. He has sent me to proclaim freedom for the prisoners and recovery of sight for the blind, to release the oppressed, to proclaim the year of the Lord's favor."

Once, as Jesus was speaking to a large crowd in Capernaum, a paralytic carried by his four friends came to him for healing. The room was so crowded that they climbed the roof, dug through the top and lowered him down right in front of Jesus. Jesus said to the man, "Son your sins are forgiven." Then, pleased with such faith, he healed the man. Jesus knew that the man needed more than a physical healing, he needed a release from his guilt. In Jewish culture of the first century a man in a crippled condition was considered guilty of something. By Jesus saying, "Your sins are forgiven you" he was healing the man at a deeper level.

These problem areas almost always stem from the person's poor relationship with God and their inability to sense his love for them. Jesus said, "If you hold to my teaching, you are really my disciples. Then you will know the truth and the truth will set you free." The kind of truth Jesus was referring to was a truth found in an abundant relationship with Christ, and an increasing sense of his love. As we minister to people with problems the answer will always be an increased quality in their relationship to God. In counseling we should help people in prayer to resolve guilt, forgive others, repent of rebellion and pride, and listen to the Holy Spirit's voice of encouragement and assurance.

It's God's nature to resist the proud but draw near to the humble in heart. Those with areas of pride and rebellion find it hard to sense God's love and presence, but those who have come to a place of surrender seem to enjoy a close relationship with God, and a sense of his love for them. It's God's love which becomes the healing factor for their brokenness and pain.

Unforgiveness must be resolved before we are able to sense God's forgiveness. Lies must be replaced with truth for the person to properly understand God's love and their freedom in Christ. When a person repents of rebellion and pride he invites a closer relationship with God. The other day a fellow came to see me because the week before he had suddenly fallen into sin. Along with this situation he also had a myriad of other problems. Much more than we could solve that day. During our conversation he mentioned some feelings of guilt which had bothered him for years. So as we closed the session, I shared 1 John 1:9 and encouraged him with God's promise to forgive. As he prayed a simple, "Father, forgive me for I have sinned," the tears began to fall as he sensed God's grace. This was the real problem. Why do seemingly good Christians fall suddenly into sin? Because inside something is unresolved with God and it's only a matter of time before they fail in their walk. Once these root causes are addressed he is able to live as a whole person and lapses into sin decrease.

How Jesus Trained Men For The Ministry

Jesus trained his disciple informally. The amazing thing to realize is that these are the men Jesus would trust to bring the gospel to the whole world. On the surface it may be difficult to understand how such an awesome and important task was left to an informal means.

But actually the informal training is much more powerful than the formal. Why? Because the informal involves a relationship of trust and love in which values can be established in the disciple. Values have to do with our hearts, our commitments, and our loyalties to the ministry. Values tell us what's important and how to best fulfill our ministries. Methods flow out of values systems. Value based discipleship is almost impossible in a classroom setting.

In the informal approach Jesus spent time with his disciples. The Bible says "he was with them." Time with a person is required because it allows you to enter their experience. These experiences are the true teachers of the disciple. As a disciple faces a situation or problem the teacher can guide the pupil along. This is the deepest level of learning possible.

When I was a youth pastor at a former church, the staff including the senior pastor, went surfing on Mondays together. These relationships greatly contributed to my personal spiritual growth.

Another way Jesus trained his disciples was by sending them into real life ministry situations. Five aspects to Jesus' method are worth noting:

1. He challenged them to step out.
2. He sent them two by two and not alone.
3. He instructed them before they left.
4. He encouraged them upon their return.
5. He took this opportunity to teach his disciples a lesson.

This last aspect seems to be at the heart of his method. As much as possible, Jesus endeavored to relate his teaching to a real life situation. In this particular case the disciples had just returned from a mission around Israel. They were overjoyed because demonic forces were subject to them. Jesus seized the moment saying, "do not rejoice that the spirits are subject to you, but rejoice that your names are written in Heaven." In this he was teaching his values. This kind of teaching situation would have never been possible unless they had a real life experience.

We can't depend on classroom education to achieve maturity in people's lives because it can't communicate a real experience. In our ministries we must challenge people beyond what they can believe for themselves. We must encourage team ministry which dissipates the fears that keep so many from ministry. We must be careful to train our people, encourage them upon each success, and take advantage of those natural teaching moments.

His Priority of Prayer

Jesus' priority in ministry was prayer. Prayer kept him strong and focused. Four points need to be made about Jesus' prayer life:

1. Prayer was the source of his strength.
2. Prayer had priority over ministry.
3. Prayer was how he made important decisions.
4. Prayer was his life style.

On one occasion, upon hearing of John the Baptist's death, Jesus withdrew to a private place for prayer. Prayer was where Jesus found strength in difficult times. Even if his schedule was overwhelming at times he maintained a healthy prayer life. Before he officially appointed the twelve he spent a night in prayer. The next morning, returning from the mountains, he choose the twelve. Prayer was how Jesus made decisions. Prayer was his lifestyle. He prayed at his baptism, at Gethsemane, on the Mount of transfiguration, in the lonely places, in the storm, with his disciples, and on the cross. He lived in constant prayer.

Today, we have such busy schedules we fail to pray. If we remain prayerless for long our ministry can become unfulfilling and burdensome. The major contributors to a bad prayer life are, distractions, busyness, laziness, and unbelief.   When we resist these, and devote ourselves to prayer, we begin to sense Christ's presence,wisdom, and power in our lives and ministries.

His Strategy For Ministry

When Christ had finished his ministry on earth he left 120 disciples behind to carry on his work.   The size of the congregation was not exceptionally large because at that point Jesus was not concerned with size, he was more concerned with the quality of each person's life. This is because his objective was not limited to his personal ministry on earth. His objective was to invest in a group who would touch the lives of people all over the world. This is why he devoted himself to just twelve and not to everyone. It was important for him to focus on a few, spending personal time, and developing quality disciples. We must not sacrifice our ministry of discipleship to our leaders. Their ministries will out last ours, that deserves our investment. We all value the exciting large group events, and these have their place, but many times the ministry becomes event oriented. We must remain people oriented.

This kind of strategy gives the small church pastor a powerful motivation, and can serve as encouragement when his church hasn't grown lately. For no matter the size of his ministry there will always be a few he is called to disciple and send forth. A pastor living in a less populated region, or pastoring in a difficult country like Japan, may take heart knowing that the few he invests in, will ultimately touch many others.

Jesus' Motivation In Ministry

Jesus' motivation in ministry was to please the Father. He spoke of his motive when he said, "I always do what pleases him." Our motive is also to please God. When we arrive in heaven we will hear, "well done good and faithful servant, you have been faithful with few, I will make you ruler over many. Enter into the joy of your Master." Often we as pastors or lay leadership lose sight of this simple and pure promise. Our hearts become distracted with lower motivations. For example, the desire to be great in our own eyes or those of others. This results in discouragement when we compare ourselves to others, pride when we succeed, and burnout when we realize our motives are unfulfilling.

Instead we should focus on the reward. Not a reward given by an employer which is compulsory, but one given by a father which always seems to be more generous than deserved. Jesus told a parable about men who started work early in the morning while others started later in the day. Those who had only worked a few hours were paid the same as those who had worked all day. So those hired in the morning assumed they would receive more than the agreed upon wage. But the master paid them all the same. Accused of unfairness, the master replied, "Have I cheated you? Can't I, because I'm good give what I want to those who worked only a few hours? Is it unjust to be kind?" This parable teaches us that rewards and appreciation for service to God are not based on merit, but the grace of God.

In the parable of the talents Jesus gives to each man according to his ability. Some received more than others because of their ability to handle more. They are also later rewarded for their faithfulness, some greater then others. But one thing was the same, both of the faithful men received the same commendation, "well done good and faithful servant, enter into the joy of your Master." This is truly what matters to the servant of God, God's gracious commendation for our faithfulness.

To please the Master is the most important motive to remain faithful to the ministry. In difficult times, when people forsake and visions tarry, we can always remember that one day our life will please the Master.

Conclusion

Out of Jesus' philosophy and values came his methods and strategies. In our churches today we practice certain traditions, use certain methods, and hold certain values which may be foreign to Jesus style of ministry. Certainly our churches can't be carbon copies of Jesus' ministry because we live in a different time and culture. On the other hand our traditional methods must never conflict with the underlying principles of Jesus. A ministry patterned after his will result in more effective evangelism, more natural follow-up of new believers, healthier Christians, a proper motive for ministry, and multiplied ministry in the world beyond our lifetime.

PERSPECTIVES FROM A NEW KID
ON THE FOURSQUARE BLOCK

S. David Moore

When I was a kid we moved only a few times, but it was plenty enough for me. I never liked having to go through the process of learning the ways or means of gaining acceptance among a new group of kids. You go through it because you have to survive and you do learn a lot. That very real childhood experience serves as the analogy that titles this paper.

I am a relatively new kid on the block that is the International Church of the Foursquare Gospel (ICFG). I didn't attend LIFE Bible College; I didn't have any history with the denomination until our church joined in November of 1985. That may not seem new to some, but as I measure the adjustment I'm still on the way to fitting in as completely as I desire. Since associating with ICFG our congregation has been remarkably blessed, and we have grown to be one of the larger churches in the Western District. We genuinely believe ICFG is where we fit in our connection to the larger body of Christ. We want to live on the Foursquare Block.

It's a little risky to attempt to share some perspectives that might sound critical to some. (I hope I'm not just paranoid.) I honestly believe I'm sharing as an insider, a member of the family. However, I'm a family member who has the unique perspective of one who "knew not" Aimee or much of Foursquare folklore. Also, I had the benefit of experiencing church life and polity on few of the other "blocks" so to speak. I submit my perspectives to the readers of this paper as just what they are: the thoughts of one pastor who is adjusting to the Foursquare culture. I do want to be honest in sharing my concerns and suggestions to stimulate thought and discussion.

Some more history will be helpful. I'm a true Christian mongrel. Saved during the Jesus movement in a charismatic Baptist ministry, I was a member early on in the church of the Nazarene. Next, I was part of a wild and legalistic Pentecostal church that I thankfully escaped. From

1976 to 1984, I was a part of the controversial Discipleship/Shepherding movement led by Bob Mumford and Charles Simpson among others. The church I now pastor was pioneered as a part of that movement. In 1984, I and our small church, withdrew from the Discipleship movement due to its extremes and imbalances. I corresponded during this time with Jack Hayford, who extended to me the invitation to relate to The Church On The Way as a part of their extension ministries. Eleven months later we joined ICFG.

I have felt warmly welcomed in so many ways. Fred Wymore, the soon retiring Western District Supervisor has been gracious and loving. We have enjoyed warm fellowship with many leaders in our area. I am refreshed by the openness and passion of our president John Holland and blessed by the strategic appointments of a younger generation of leaders like Don Long, our new General Supervisor. The LEAD program to develop and strengthen leaders is commendable and valuable to our future.

Having said this, there remains a certain struggle I must acknowledge. This comes back to the analogy with which I opened the paper. I feel accepted in some ways, but it seems I'm still perceived as not being fully Foursquare (Call me Threesquare! Forgive the pun.) Part of this is, I'm sure, the struggle of adjusting to a new polity, learning the heroes and the history, and allowing time to acclimate. But I would be less than honest to say that's all it is.

Let me just say it. I wonder at times if it isn't: "All Foursquare leaders are Foursquare, only some are more Foursquare than others." Please don't shoot me yet. I don't believe this is intentional. It just seems that those who have attended LIFE, started their ministry in our movement, or who have historic or relational ties to ICFG are perceived as more Foursquare than someone who joins midstream with no previous Foursquare connection. Let me say again I have felt most welcomed; it's just that at times I am very aware I'm "adopted" into the family.

This isn't said to accuse anyone or impugn motives, and I believe many of our leaders at Headquarters would not realize it is part of the environment of ICFG. I realize that what I am writing approximates the genre of the back alley conversations that can be critical and subjective. That is certainly not my intent.

My concern is that ICFG leaders like myself need to find more than just an identification beyond our local churches. There needs to be full and complete welcome into the Foursquare family. Our movement is being blessed wonderfully as many leaders join us after already establishing their ministries. Commendably, we welcome this and warmly so. However does our movement extend to adopted members the full rights and privileges it extends to those who are more historically and relationally Foursquare? Are the same leadership opportunities available to adopted members? For example, the denominational presidency is open only to Foursquare Bible College graduates. Are the perspectives of adopted leaders sought and weighed with as equal value? The questions are worthy of consideration at the least.

The Need For Dynamic Structures

This honest, and somewhat tongue in cheek, observation serves to bring to fore the larger issue and what is my real focus. We live in a very different world today than when our movement was born and established. In 1995, we as a denomination are very different. We are a melting pot of the new, the old, and the in between. We have leaders trained in the Foursquare system, and those trained in other systems. Additionally, we serve an increasingly diverse constituency. As a movement, we are faced with new and demanding responsibilities to respond to these changes. We are in the pains of transition and my struggle as a new kid on the block to fit is just a symptom of that transition.

My genuine conviction is that our movement is attempting to evaluate the issues and to make the necessary adjustments to secure our future. This is evidenced by John Holland's passion for relevance and his desire to be in touch and hear from our local church pastors. Further, I realize that larger structures and systems change with a painful slowness that calls for patience toward our denominational leaders. The more centrally governed the larger organization is only compounds the problems more. Our movement faces a great challenge because our polity is tilted toward centralization.

Christian leaders who are reading current literature and halfway aware of secular management trends have heard of the term paradigm shift. The rethinking of structures, methods and means is reshaping many of the assumptions and monoliths of our contemporary culture. The church is being confronted with the same need for new paradigms. The call to contextualize our message and rethink our structures is coming from a broad spectrum of Christian leaders. This is a stretching time for those of us who lead, particularly denominational leaders who face the enormous risks and struggles in dealing with the larger, historic church structures.

I am absolutely convinced that church structure is one of the most essential and basic issues in reaching our generation for Christ. Far too often the church has held onto the methods and structures that have hindered the Gospel. The mandate to evangelize and disciple requires confrontation with whatever holds back our task. We face a great challenge in the West with the clear emergence of a neo-pagan, post-Christian culture. As Stephen Carter's book title declares, we live in The Culture of Disbelief.

Refreshing changes are apparent in churches like Willow Creek Community and others, and the success of these new paradigms has created a surge to get on the band wagon of change. However, leaders in the church must evaluate the need for change not simply to copy success, but to capture the heart of mission. We need to again understand the nature of the church and its implications on our methods, modes and structures.

The church is relationally based. We are not primarily an organization, but a community of believers under the dynamic Lordship of Jesus Christ. Few would deny this definition, yet when it comes to our praxis, it is easy to accept status quo rather than embrace the conflict that change so often requires. However painful it is, seeing the church as a charismatic community demands confrontation with structures and systems that impose static, organizational restrictions on the dynamic nature of the church. In Robert Cobbles overlooked book, The Church and the Powers: A Theology of Church Structure, he says: "Church structure has an immediate and dramatic impact on the life and mission of the church." Our movement must boldly and brutally evaluate our structures in the light of the new day in which we live.

A Biblical Perspective

What follows answers to something of the passion I have to impose a Biblical paradigm to our structures and systems. Let me acknowledge that we do need structure and organization for the purpose of serving our mission; further, there is always tension for any denomination or organization between its commitment to respect tradition and heritage and the need for dynamic change. Importantly though, let us remember Aimee Semple MacPherson's purpose for founding the ICFG was mission based. Our by-laws say our organizational structures were set in place to provide for credentialing and training ministers, establishing local churches and training centers, and joint missionary enterprise. Our focus then must be on how to realize these objectives in our unique contemporary setting and to recognize the environmental changes within our own movement. A quest for relevance expresses the essence of the ongoing fulfillment of our founder's vision. Aimee was a radical innovator, and let's keep that heritage alive.

I might add that I am very aware of the great liberty our movement gives local congregations to find their own unique ministry personalities and that many Foursquare churches and leaders are blazing an innovative trail. I trust it's evident than I am seeking to address our larger structures and systems that tie us together.

I want to make a brief Biblical appeal to set a context for the more practical suggestions I want to make. I recognize that the New Testament gives us no precise form for church structures and government; rather, it presents broad principles that allow for varied application within existing structures. With the following Scriptures I seek to present a more relationally focused paradigm for church government and ministry training that hopefully will help us as a movement think through our present structures.

In Acts 20:13-38, we have the narrative of Paul's farewell to the Ephesian elders. What marks the passage in my view is not just Paul's loving charge, but the emotional response at the end of the passage. The text says that the elders "wept as they embraced him and kissed him". What grieved them most was his statement that they would never see him again. This is interesting! I don't know that I've seen many leaders relate this passionately together. (Some leaders would be glad to never again see one of their denominational leaders.) Paul and these elders loved each other, and I believe we are seeing here something of the consequence of a relational and less structural model of church leadership. This was not a ministerial association; these were men functioning within a loving community of shared leadership.

Consider Paul's apostolic approach. He founded the church at Ephesus and stayed over two years training and developing the leaders there (Acts 19:10). Paul stayed at Corinth for eighteen months grounding the church (Acts 18:11). Paul traveled with a kind of apostolic band of which Barnabas, Silas, Luke, Timothy, and Titus are but a few who seem to have been influenced and discipled by Paul. Most scholars agree that the New Testament uses the terms pastor, elder and bishop interchangeably. Paul appoints pastor/elders out from the local church and recommends others do the same. (Acts 14:23; I Tim. 3; Titus 1. I could make an apologetic here with supporting documentation, but this is not my purpose. I hope the readers are aware of the arguments that have been made exegetically for the synonymous use of the terms mentioned above.)

Paul's letters are not mere theological treatises, they are filled with personal comments and references to specific people. His love and passion are clear as he describes how he prays and worries about the people and the churches he cares for. He describes being personally refreshed by those who have come to him with news about the churches he loves, and he also expresses the pain and disappointment in very personal ways of those who have betrayed or deserted him.

His letters hardly sound like they are written to people he has nothing more than ecclesiastical authority over; instead, he seems to appeal to them out of relationship versus structure. As an example:

> "I am not writing this to shame you, but to warn you, as my dear children. Even though you have ten thousand guardians in Christ, you do not have many fathers, for in Christ Jesus I became your father through the gospel. Therefore I urge you to imitate me." (I Cor. 4:14-16)

Particularly powerful are his comments about Timothy.

> "For this reason I am sending to you Timothy, my son whom I love, who is faithful in the Lord. He will remind you of my way of life in Christ Jesus, which agrees with what I teach everywhere in every church." (I Cor. 4:17)
>
> "I hope in the Lord Jesus to send Timothy to you soon, that I also may be cheered when I receive news about you. I have no one else like him, who takes a genuine interest in your welfare. For everyone looks out for his own interests, not those of Jesus Christ. But you know that Timothy has proved himself, because as a son with his father he has served with me in the work of the gospel. I hope, therefore, to send him as soon as I see how things go with me." (Phil 2:19-23).

Add to this his emotion filled second letter to Timothy and the deeply personal and transparent second letter to the Corinthians. In all the above I see a man very much leading from an honest, relational, and personal mentoring paradigm. This I do not believe was Paul's grand plan for church structure, but was simply a result of his seeing the church as a network of relationships under Christ's Lordship. In the Pauline materials I see several broad principles and it would serve us to consider their implications on our denominational and local structures for training, supporting and relating as leaders.

What are these broad principles?

1. In the New Testament ministry training is primarily relationally focused rather than institutionally focused.

2. Leadership training is primarily local church based.

3. Personal mentoring was normative in developing leaders.

4. New Testament church government was comprised of established leaders who functioned together in a supportive community.

5. These leaders exercised clear authority and chain of command.

At this point I want to acknowledge that our movement is rich in relationships. In the Western District, of which I am a part we often refer to the family like relationships we share. In our Bible colleges students experience mentoring relationships with professors. Our denominational leaders love and genuinely care for the pastors and people in our movement. This is a blessing. Yet, we must ask ourselves: how well do our larger structures serve and fit these Biblical principles? What can we do to more closely approximate a Biblical model? Are any of our structures becoming outdated because of contemporary cultural changes and more specific ICFG environmental changes? Answering these questions is the challenge we must face.

Some Radical Propositions

Now comes the insanity and presumption of the new kid on the block. I'd like to propose some very practical responses to the above principles as they touch ICFG. They are not a blueprint for revolution or rebellion, they are merely ideas to be weighed. Personally, I have never been one who likes to be criticized without having any suggestions given to answer concerns. This is my attempt to be more than just a critic but to speak as a loyal, "adopted" member of the Foursquare family. In the context of our day what then should we do?

- Moving toward decentralization.
  - Developing effective communication channels from our headquarters to local pastors is essential. Often in large organizations the central leadership is easily out of touch with what is happening in the trenches. Dr. Holland seems aware of this and has been seeking remedy on the problem. These efforts should be continued and be expanded.
  - Great effort should be given to increasing the investment of energy and resource to empowering our regional divisional

leadership. Let me again be frank about the back alley talk. I hear leaders speak of their token participation at divisional meetings to meet the attendance expectation. Some simply don't attend. Why? Often it is because little of value happens in the meetings. Personally, over the years, I've found that it's easy in these gatherings relate superficially and professionally instead of relationally and dependently. I am sure this is not true everywhere and that we have many excellent divisional leaders. Nonetheless, I've heard the complaints in many places. If structures lose their relevance they begin to be ignored or worse, mindlessly served. I believe our district and divisional approach is an excellent model provided that the divisional leaders are carefully and prayerfully selected. Excuse my ignorance but:

- Are divisional leaders given clear purpose and objectives for their task?

- Do we provide training and tools to help them with their task?

- Do we have a system to regularly evaluate their performance?

- Would it be helpful to consider having divisional leaders serve specific renewable terms?

Divisional leaders need to have the skills required to lead leaders which is no easy task. Emphasis should be made on building a loving, supportive community of leaders who share common values and common struggles.

- District offices need to develop effective support structures for pioneer churches. I have heard pastors speak of their aloneness in planting a church. (I believe the ideal model, which I mention below, is church planting from the local church since it provides a stronger and more natural, relational connection for support.) Perhaps a full time district position might be created, or a team of pastoral volunteers assembled, that would travel to small pioneer churches to provide a kind of apostolic support to the leaders through personal ministry and counsel. At the very least, a "call us if you need to" relationship must be established.

● Confronting any fortress mentality.

- None would deny that our movement has struggled as all large movements do with the battle between the old guard and the new guard. The leaders who experienced the glory of a precious heritage fight to hold on to the essence of what birthed the movement, often confusing the organizational structures and methods for that essence. The new guard rises to throw away the old structures and ways often disregarding the need for heritage. We must create forums for leaders to discuss these issues head on, and with love and respect struggle on toward the future, mutually valuing each other's perspectives. Convention business meetings are far too large and unmanageable for the frank kind of bottom line debate I believe is needed.

- It would be well to establish regional ad hoc groups of denominational leaders and local pastors, to specifically address and examine ICFG's structures and systems in the light of the contemporary setting.

● <u>Fully receive our adopted Foursquare leaders. (The new kids on the block)</u>

- Consideration should be given to recognition of years of licensed and ordained ministry service that were prior to Foursquare licensing or ordination. This would show proper honor to the faithful service in another part of Christ's body. In my view it displays a fuller acceptance of these leaders and their service that ought to be counted toward their years of service as a Foursquare minister of the gospel. Certain criteria could be established that would define how this recognition would work practically.

- ICFG should continue to consider trusted and capable adopted leaders for key positions in the larger structures such as: district supervisors, divisional superintendents, cabinet members, key committee appointments and headquarters staff positions.

- Consideration should be given to no longer requiring our president to be a graduate of a Foursquare college.

- Train and encourage district and divisional leaders to deliberately and patiently orient the adopted pastors and leaders.

● <u>Revise and adjust our ministry training models.</u>

C. Peter Wagner, well known professor of church growth and missiology at Fuller Seminary, has linked a Christian movement's vitality of ongoing mission to an emphasis on non-professional clergy. Many educators are calling for a radical revision of the current ministry training models. Space doesn't allow for an apologetic for my recommendations, and I trust it won't prove necessary for presenting them. I realize the following are the most challenging propositions of this paper.

- A new emphasis should be made on developing local church based ministry training. It is in the local church that time can be given to develop the Godly character and integrity which is the essential foundation for ministry skills. The local church is the practical place for personal mentoring of emerging leaders.

- The establishing of regional LIFE Bible College extension campuses would be very helpful in supporting local church based ministry training. The one year residency requirement for a BA. degree should be dropped so that fully external degrees are possible for students.

While I do not want to argue against the value for so many of the on campus Bible college or seminary experiences, the fact is, on average, most pastors feel their academic training did not prepare them for the rigors of ministry.

In the local church, leaders in training can learn what are the joys, pains and perils, of ministry on the front line. Educators agree that the learning curve is high when application is a part of the learning process. Through the supervision of ministry assignments and full or part-time internship, practical ministry skills can be learned.

- Church Planting by local churches should be viewed as a natural by-product of training that is local church based. As churches prepare and send leaders with church plant teams, ongoing support is simply an extension of already existing, loving relationships. Obviously, not every church will be pioneering new churches, but those who do should be encouraged, enabled, and supported.

- It is not my purpose to suggest that we close our primary Bible colleges. Great investments have been made toward facilities and faculties. Perhaps we should consider moving these schools more toward graduate education to train and equip our many gifted leaders who could take their skills back to the regional training centers and pastorates. Also, campuses and faculties could be utilized by developing modular programs consisting of one or two week intensive courses for undergraduate and graduate study.

- Continue to invest and enhance our LEAD program to benefit our "in the trench" pastors and leaders. It would be helpful to grant graduate credit or Continuing Education Units to those leaders interested in further study.

Concluding....

I fully recognize that some of my propositions are most challenging. I am sure that they are not entirely new and many have been considered before. Some are more radical than others, but all are rooted in a paradigm that fosters the dynamic nature of the church with a more relational, less centralized perspective. We do need structures, organization, and chain of command, but we must keep in mind that their aim must ultimately be to serve the release of ministry in the local church and to empower missionary effort. As I've already stated, our movement is different today and my adoption into the Foursquare movement is an example of our changing face. Our structures and systems must be elastic and flexible enough, not only to embrace "new kids", but to change with the times.

Over the centuries of church history many vital and vibrant movements have risen and fallen. God birthed each movement in answer to a cry from a needy world and a hungry church. Students of church history know also that many of these movements were not able to survive cultural changes. So far ICFG has faired reasonably well in transition and, may I say again, is uniquely poised to make the changes that will ensure our relevance to a new generation. We have a president who is seeking to be a son of Issachar, striving to know the times and what the church should do and be. Men within our movement like Jack Hayford challenge us to contend for the present glory of God in our midst. We have a rich heritage from faithful older leaders and an energetic group of young leaders. Importantly our movement has tolerated and even embraced pioneers and trailblazers who have discovered new and radical ways of doing church. This whole process has not always been comfortable or tidy; nonetheless, we have more than survived. With such history and wealth will we continue to adapt and change in answer to the present and future need? Frankly, I think we're going to make it unto a new day, but let's face it: it won't be easy! Thank God for His grace.

Further Reading....

What follows is a list of books that deal with church structure in our contemporary culture. This is not a total endorsement for the ideas and paradigms in these books. Some of these books stand in near or overt opposition to each other. Nonetheless, I have found them to be most helpful as I think through the issues.

Anderson, Leith. Dying For Change. Minneapolis: Bethany House Publishers, 1976.

Cobble, James F., Jr.. The Church and the Powers. Peabody, Mass.:Hendrickson Publishers, 1988.

Colson, Charles. The Body. Dallas: Word Publishing, 1992.

Doner, Colonel V.. The Samaritan Strategy. Brentwood, Tenn.: Wolgemuth and Hyatt, Publishers, Inc., 1988.

George, Carl F.. How To Break Growth Barriers. Grand Rapids: Baker Book House, 1993.

————. Prepare Your Church for the Future. Tarrytown, New York: Fleming H. Revell Co., 1991.

Guiness, Os.. Dining With The Devil. Baker Book House, 1993.

Guiness, Os and Steel, John eds., No God But God. Chicago: Moody Press, 1992.

Hunter, George G. III. To Spread the Power. Nashville: Abingdon Press, 1987.

Jacobsen, Wayne. The Naked Church. Eugene, Ore.: Harvest House Publishers, 1987.

Logan, Robert E.. Beyond Church Growth. Old Tappan, New Jersey: Flemming H. Revell Co., 1989.

Martin, Glen & McIntosh, Gary. The Issachar Factor. Nashville: Broadman and Holman Publishers, 1993.

Neighbour, Ralph W. Jr.. Where Do We Go From Here?. Houston: Touch Publications, Inc., 1990.

Peterson, Eugene H.. Under the Unpredictable Plant. Grand Rapids: William B. Eerdmans Publishing Co., 1992.

Shelley, Bruce & Shelley, Marshall. The Consumer Church. Downers Grove, Illinois: Inter - Varsity Press, 1992.

Snyder, Howard A.. The Community of the King. Downers Grove, Illinois: Inter - Varsity Press, 1977.

————. The Problem of Wine Skins. Downers Grove, Illinois: Inter -
   Varsity Press, 1976.

————. The Radical Wesley. Downers Grove, Illinois: Inter-Varsity
   Press, 1980.

Webster, Douglas D.. Selling Jesus. Downers Grove, Illinois: Inter -
   Varsity Press, 1992.

EQUIPPING MINISTRY
IN SEARCH OF A MODEL

Ralph Moore

The Foursquare Church is hot. Our pastors are published in books and Christian magazines. Our songwriters affect the worship patterns of a nation. With a certain irony, our Pentecostal theology is now seen as a refreshing and mature solution to a century-old battle over spiritual gifts. Moreover, we are planting churches at a rate that makes us one of the fastest growing movements in America.

We've survived three generations without compromising our message. We've had the wisdom to benefit from a couple of revivals beyond the one that birthed us. Our leaders counterbalance bravery and caution with ease, allowing us to think radically and move rationally. We've stood apart from the mainstream while reaching for the scriptural balance our founder craved. Trouble is, success breeds complacency. We need light footed thinkers to pack our success into muscle instead of fat.

REVOLUTIONARY INSIGHTS

Historic turning points are easily overlooked. Henry Ford is the "father of the modern assembly line." But, few remember him as the genius that sparked a revolution in family finance and created today's huge credit industry.[1] By raising wages and lowering the cost of cars Ford gave every workingman the opportunity to become a car owner. Car loans paved the way for cheap credit and long mortgages, jarring American history and culture forever.

Christopher Columbus was another history-bending visionary. His genius lay not in the roundness of the planet. Many acknowledged that. Columbus broke fear and tradition by willfully sailing out of the sight of land. In a daring search for an alternate route to Japan, he discovered the New World. Free thinking sailors and entrepreneurs immediately began poking for a way around, under or through it. They focused on the short cut to Asia. It took 200 years for people to postulate that what they found was more important than what they were looking for.

History of Foursquare Licensing

Ford built a bigger market and Columbus found a bigger world; we excavated a legion of new pastors. Our denomination began with one mother church and a slew of homegrown leaders. Zeal and the baptism in the Holy Spirit were the key requisites to leadership. We started churches like wildfire. The death of our founder touched off a period of grief and painful self examination. That process included a shift to the traditional pattern of a four year Bible College requirement for ministry. This narrowed the gate, nearly halting the planting of churches and the growth of the movement.

During the Charismatic Revival/ Jesus Movement many churches returned to the Angelus Temple model, appointing laymen to staff positions. The inevitable happened when fast growing churches ventured into reproduction with men they had trained in-house. These church planters lacked legal credentials for ministry. In 1973, denominational leaders responded with a far reaching decision to receive these men and women into ministry through a multi-tiered licensing system.

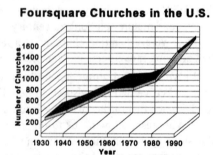

Foursquare Churches in the U.S.

It has taken two decades of expansion to realize that what we got was more important than what we were looking for. The decision to license laypastors opened the door for wholesale midlife career change among mature men. It gave us access to men who had been on the planet long enough to have their house visibly in order. Today laypastors account for more than half of those ministering in our churches. We've returned to our roots and grow accordingly. We found a new category of labor for the harvest.

THE IDENTIFYING MISSION OF A BIBLE SCHOOL

There are those who would destroy this resource and recast the Bible school as the "hole in the hourglass." On the other hand, a radical itinerant evangelist I once heard suggested he would blow up every Bible college and seminary in the land. We need balance between our old methods and the new. The schools are an absolute necessity but we cannot live without the laypastors. Is there a way these two systems can enhance each other? Before we attempt a marriage between the two, we should examine the mission and value of the Bible school. We should also look for biblical precedent for our methods, whatever they may be.

I recently received a call from a friend. He was involved in a headquarters discussion about licensing pastors for Foursquare churches. It seems an influential businessman in one of our churches had complained that his child was attending LIFE Bible College (at dad's expense) to get a pastor's license. A staff pastor in his home church held license by virtue of his responsibility. The man was frustrated that the staffer held license without expending the time or money required by this businessman and his offspring. He saw us giving away 'free' licenses. I was called because my two children attend the Bible school while our church is a heavy user of the lay licenses. My friend wanted my opinion as a user of those free licenses and a buyer of those won by hard work in the classroom. I reminded him of apples and oranges.

False Pillars

A Bible college educates people in the scriptures and provide hands-on training opportunities for ministry. It serves well when allowed to function as a gift to the church, but not when called upon to serve as a singular entrypoint into ministry. Credentials for ministry are the joint bailiwick of the Holy Spirit and the judicatory structure of the denomination.

To cast the college as the fount of licensing authority (like the businessman above) is to build a bridge on weak pylons. The system which does so makes several key mistakes about the training process:

1. Confuses education with the Holy Spirit. Credentialing is His role. The apostles and self-taught giants like G. Campbell Morgan are joined by everyday people who would grow up under His guidance within the ranks of a local church. Where would we be without Daniel Brown?

2. Confuses classroom ability with the ability to minister life to others. A diploma is earned by diligent study, good writing, and an ability to take tests. It does not insure the compassion, leadership skill, or spiritual gifts requisite to ministry. The school can enhance a minister, it cannot create one.

3. Ignores the law of reproduction as it applies to discipleship. All creatures reproduce in kind. When making disciples, we reproduce ourselves. This applies to professors as much as pastors. A pastor will build a value system into the life of those he mentors. A professor will do the same. The difficulty lies with the application of those values in the local church; one set fits easily while the other requires careful adaptation.

4. Misses the order of events attached to Paul's model of evangelism. The Apostle Paul left a legacy of evangelistic strategy as he traveled the Mediterranean world. He declared the gospel, made converts, and immediately began the discipling process. He quickly organized churches, appointing his new disciples as elders. In Acts 14, he appointed some people after only two weeks of personal contact.[2] Finally, he continued to disciple or educate these people *in place* through friendship and letters. The education was continuing rather than initiating while credentials were based on the obvious ability to lead.

5. Forces unrealistic goals on the school. More Bible college and seminary graduates drop out of ministry than continue after the first two years. If the college is held responsible for populating all our pulpits, it can only fail. If seen as an adjunct to a larger system, it is an emphatic success. Fully embracing off-campus continuing education would afford rampant opportunity to bless the churches.

6. Locks out proven success. By virtue of age, family responsibility and personal achievement, the midlife recruit is tethered to his locale. Those characteristics which deem him a worthy candidate also tie him to an income source as well as to the ministry that spawned him. Bible school as the gateway to a license geographically eliminates this person from pastoral ministy. If seen through the experience of the Foursquare Church over the past 20 years, such a loss is unthinkable.

The arguments about schooling also concern the quality of education. They are hardly new, Lyle Schaller states that "those who today complain that too much education can ruin a person for the pastoral ministry are echoing a five-hundred-year-old cry."[3] He goes on to note that specialization and increased education have not produced a measurably better product in medicine, law, education or clergy and have only succeeded in pricing many out of the market.[4]

Schaller's arguments place our movement at the vanguard. He says the trend of the future is toward pastors and leaders raised up by mentoring or local church training systems and a move back to the ministry as a perceived vocation or calling rather, than a profession as it stands today.[5] Others note that current clergy training and compensation practices work in the suburbs but fail in the inner cities and in sparsely populated rural areas.[6]

Real Values in a Bible College Education

None of this is to reduce the value of a Bible college or seminary. The more education the better. It is the *role* of the school that should be examined. Here are three irreplaceable benefits provided by formal schooling:

1. Stabilizer to the parent organization. Clothing styles may come and go on campus. But theological fads and ministry gimmicks have a hard time penetrating the thinking, teaching and writing of faithful professors. Thus, the school assumes a role as keeper of core doctrines of the movement.

2. The rich heritage of the campus experience. Years spent together in dorms and classrooms generate a network of future leaders for the denominational family. Shared experiences forge ties for the inevitable in-service leadership pyramid. Locally-trained leadership can never provide this organic infrastructure so necessary to our future.

3. A reproducible educational experience. The classroom trained pastor is positioned, and called to duplicate his knowledge in others. He has been given much and much is required. The school can graduate people who see themselves as walking seminaries. As these people disseminate their knowledge to a handful of disciples, they create another round of laypastors. Every graduate can and should duplicate himself in a dozen or so people in the course of a lifetime.

IN SEARCH OF A MODEL

If we are to expand our options we will want to take advantage of both training structures. We certainly won't take the position of that short-sighted businessman or the evangelist I mentioned earlier. But, our options must be biblical.

Searching the Scriptures

Jesus and the twelve provide the baseline model. His training of the apostles was highly relational, offered a low teacher-to-student ratio, provided immediate hands-on experience, and is easy to reproduce. It should be and has become our *primary* method of training for ministry. But, it should not be the only model for training.

The Book of Acts offers six church planting models for our consideration, each one hints at the training of its leadership:

- The first mention of church activity in chapter two suggests house-to-house meetings following a large celebration, approximated in today's *Meta-Church* teaching. House leaders followed up the large group teaching of the apostles in an informal setting. The preaching of the apostles was the primary training tool for leaders.

- The second incidence of church planting is what I call *Controlled Pragmatic Expansion*. The saints ran for their lives in Acts 8. But, everywhere they went they preached what they knew. Here also the primary training agency was the teaching of the apostles. The difference is that the learners had to follow through and act like pastors without much choice in the matter.

- *Spontaneous Combustion* describes the birth of the church in Ethiopia. The eunuch had some knowledge of the Old Testament but needed the correction and instruction of Philip to know the Lord. Without further instruction he took the gospel home and Christianized a culture.

- *Rapid Itinerant Birthing* of churches followed Paul and his teams. They preached, discipled for a pitifully short time, and then organized churches around hastily appointed leadership. The preponderance of training came afterward as is apparent through the writing of those training manuals, the epistles.

- *Primary Location-Daily Discipleship* (a Bible school) is mentioned just once, but with astounding effect. When Paul retreated to the school of Tyrannus with just a few disciples he remained for two years. The result was that all who lived in Asia Minor heard the gospel.

- Finally we see evidence of favoritism or *Single Minded Mentoring* when Paul selected Silas and Timothy over John Mark and Barnabas. Strong relational communication of truth, much like the relationship of Jesus to the twelve, may seem exclusive as it rewards likemindedness and productivity in the disciple.

God is flexible and we should work at it. Biblical models are many and varied . We should keep all of them in our toolkit. New Testament leaders were marked by four qualifiers: a calling, spiritual gifts appropriate to that calling, followers (you are not a leader without them), and ongoing input.

Modern Equivalents

It is fruitless to quibble about Biblical foundations if they cannot be made to work in our day and culture. If our models are truly biblical and alive, we ought to be able to find them in someone other than ourselves.

Learning from the Baptists

Seminary as the threshold to pastoral ministry is a recent innovation in the United States. Prior to the establishment of seminaries, there were three predominant training patterns for pastoral ministry: Congregational and Presbyterian churches used a system of apprenticeship following college. Methodist in-service training coupled circuit-riding apprentice preachers and lay leaders in home meetings. The circuit rider who was being discipled by a more established pastor showed up for one sermon a month, the lay leader did the actual pastoring and ran the rest of the meetings. Finally, Baptists in the south ran their *tent-making ministries.* This was used most effectively in the South and on the frontier. [7]

After the Methodists, Baptists offered the least formal training. They often merely chose the most gifted man in the congregation. This occurred with or without the support of the neighboring churches. The system allowed for rapid proliferation of churches.[8] Because Christian influence was weak on the frontier, the Baptists were best positioned to make a difference. Their rapid-fire expansion overwhelmed the surrounding unstructured and violent society. Unburdened by the educational costs and time constraints of the other movements, they also enjoyed the advantage of a pastor who reflected the culture of his parishioners.[9] The less formal the educative process, the faster the growth. Baptists would recruit a man based on giftedness and desire. No attempt at formal training was required of a church planter or pastor away from the big cities. The Southern Baptists far outstripped the others in the number of congregations and their membership numbers are just as impressive as their growth of congregations, having gone from 100,000 members in the year 1800 to 20,000,000 by 1960.[10]

It is important to note that Baptist churches, particularly the Southern Baptists, have built some of the finest colleges and seminaries in this country. But they did not fall prey to limiting access to the ministry to those high-threshold operations. While building scholastic institutions, they strictly protect the concept of the locally-trained and lay-led mission church. In fact, many seminarians adopt and act out the mission model concurrent with their classroom experience. The processes we developed in Foursquare by near accident in 1973 are at the root of the success of Baptist churches in the United States.

Comparison of Growth among Congregationalists, Methodists and Baptists in the United States from 1750-1950.[11]

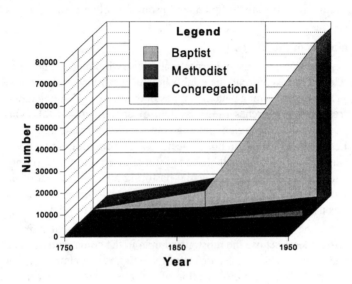

YEAR	1750	1850	1950
Congregational	600 churches	1,600 churches	3,200 churches
Methodist	0 churches	1,200 churches	5,800 churches
Baptist	200 churches	8,600 churches	77,000 churches

Missionary wisdom

Any system we adopt ought to reflect a certain universality. It should be supra-cultural and not just the product of our own local or national interests. Foursquare missionaries have long built upon the shoulders of lay-trained pastors while building Bible schools adjacent to large founding churches. Oversees, they've used schools to generate *extension programs* for those trained in the trenches. Missionaries use every means available to them but often question the use of lay pastors in a developed nation like the U.S. or Japan.

Our own measurable success and that of the Baptists in the U.S. puts that fear to rest. A look toward Japan provides more food for thought. Japan displays an inverse evidence of the value of seminary education. The Japanese sustain the most highly-educated and professionally-paid clergy in the world while showing little in terms of results.[12] While Japanese national church growth (with a professionally-trained clergy) has been among the slowest in the world, the country shows great success wherever lay led movements work in conjunction with Bible school trained leadership.[13] In days gone by, the only real revival the country ever had bore witness to the effectiveness of locally-trained clergy and the ensuing spontaneous multiplication of churches.[14]

OPPORTUNITY KNOCKS

We always want to make a good thing better, but what really is better? As we face the 21st century, what can we do to insure optimum contribution to the Kingdom of God? How can we best do our part when it comes to the Great Commission? We will probably avoid the pitfall of pulling back licensing authority from the churches and repositioning it in the hands of the Bible schools, but avoiding mistakes is merely neutral leadership. What can we do positively? Imagine we were living five centuries ago: the agenda in Columbus' day should have been to forske what they were seeking and take advantage of what they found. Here are some possibilities raised by those who loosened the reigns two decades ago:

1. Take a lesson from the Southern Baptists: build the best institutions we can while protecting the pathway of informal training and spontaneous lifting into ministry. Do not restrict the process with requirements beyond discipleship and the confidence of local elders. Also, offer more and better training options to the more than 50 percent of our pastors who have not had the benefit of formal training. Leave these as options, do not construct a new and higher threshold to ministry.

2. Expand the role of our Bible colleges. We should view our colleges as parents for in-service training. The schools could provide scaled down curriculum and function as an accrediting agency for locally operated in-service training. Videotaped classes coupled with a live discussion leader and proxy could extend classroom boundaries. LIFE Bible College of Canada already does this with ever expanding success.

3. Raise our sights. We have incredible tools for planting and operating churches if we take advantage of the mid-life calling. We should plan for 4000 churches by 2015. We should anticipate congregations in closer proximity in order to fully saturate communities with our influence.

4. *Target the inner city and cross cultural opportunities awaiting us.* Many seasoned laymen would start a house church in their own immigrant culture or inner-city neighborhood. They will never do it if we *require* the expense and time necessary for a campus experience. Our history shows we can enlist them if we are willing to acknowledge the gifts and work of the Holy Spirit in their lives. At this point we must identify and eliminate several growth-restricting obstacles in our thinking. The educational process is not the only mental barrier to growth. We must begin to admit the value of a congregation if it meets regularly with as few as 30 people (our own charter requirement). We should not await the acquisition of property to view a congregation as *normal.* Finally, discussions limiting the credential of a bivocational pastor are absurd. A man with a secular income is saving us money, not hurting our prestige. He provides a capital base for opportunities we could not otherwise embrace.

5. *Anticipate some breakage.* There will be some failures involving lay-trained pastors. They will be held up as examples of proof of the need for formal training. However, for every example of an informally trained failure you wouldn't have to search hard to find a parallel example among our formally trained brethren. In fact, the dropout rate of the formally trained pastor is much higher than that of those with in-service training. Neither system is superior and both are necessary to achieve our goals.

Final Concerns

For in-service training to work, it must feel practical to the end user. Any system must see its students as clients and customers. We can't give them whatever we *think* they need, they will only buy what they *feel* they need. The pressing need is for laborers to participate in the harvest. Any tools we provide that labor force must be flexible in schedule and content. They should be built around a small workgroup rather than a large classroom experience. This allows for a relational experience, provides a low teacher-to-pupil ratio, and permits the pastor of a small church to use the materials provided. Curriculum should be designed for busy people, since most users will have a full time job, a family, meaningful ministry and little time for study. This is not to imply simplistic curriculum, but materials designed for the "hit-and-run" student working during coffee breaks and late at night.

Any new program must equip for ministry, not exclude from ministry. Under the guise of providing credentials, we too often discredit those who didn't participate in our program. Tools must be enhancers, not barriers to ministry if we would succeed at the great commission.

Finally, we must design curriculum to *follow after* the commencement of meaningful ministry. People already doing the ministry are hungriest to sharpen their skills. Those merely contemplating ministry should be challenged to do something before they are ever allowed to take a class.

NOTES

1. Robert Lacey, *Ford: The Men and the Machine,*(New York: Ballentine Books, 1986), pp. 320-321.

2. Acts 13:13-52; 14:23

3. Lyle E. Schaller, *It's A Different World* (Nashville: Abingdon Press, 1987), p. 198.

4. Schaller, pp.200-211.

5. Lyle E. Schaller, *The Senior Minister* (Nashville: Abingdon Press, 1990), p. 84,85.

6. Mulholland, pp, 9,10.

7. Kenneth B. Mulholland, *Adventures in Training the Ministry: a Honduran case study in theological education by extension* (Nutley, NJ: Presbyterian and Reformed Publishing Co., 1976), pp. 4,5.

8. Mulholland, p. 8.

9. John Dillenberger and Claude Welch, *Protestant Christianity Interpreted Through Its Development* (New York: Charles Scribner's Sons, 1954), p. 148.

10. Edwin Scott Gaustad, *Historical Atlas of Religion in America* (New York: Harper and Row, 1962), p.55.

11. Braun, p. 55.

12. Otis Cary, *Protestant Missions*, Vol. II of *A History of Christianity in Japan*, (Tokyo: Charles E. Tuttle Company, 1976), pp. 163, 296.

13. Author's observations of Japanese Christian movements include: a)Shalom churches under Pastor Elmer Inafuku with 10 large congregations in 22 years. b) New Life churches led by Pastor Mizuno with 19 congregations in the same time frame, using the same principles. Pastor David Masui of Hakodate Zion Kyokai has used this method to raise pastors and plant nearly a dozen churches in his own and other church families.

14. Cary, pp. 171, 320.

ARE WE A BUSINESS OR ARE WE THE CHURCH?
or
Have We Become So Business-Minded We're No Heavenly Good?

Ron Pinkston

DECLARING MY PURPOSE

I purposely titled this paper with a question because it is my desire to bring up as many questions as I may answer. It is not a question I ask lightly or rhetorically. I do not think the question is simple. However, in this fast paced, high powered, get results decade, I would suggest that to not bring up or attempt to answer this question could be a potentially serious mistake because the business world has unquestionably become a part of the church's thinking, effecting its cultural language, its methodologies of governing, its styles of leadership, and much more. Yet, to my knowledge there has been little if any meaningful analysis of those effects in terms of drawing the church closer to Christ or further away.

And, I believe there is plenty of ambiguity to go around in the church on this subject. Even George Barna, the consummate student of the church's effectiveness, sounds unsure when he writes, "Is the business model for evaluation the right comparison for what we do in the church? Maybe, maybe not." In short, that seems a good description of church leaders' attitudes also, when the point is pressed...maybe, maybe not.

So, this article is designed to press the point in hopes that the reader will be encouraged to challenge the introduction of business principles into the church and not accept them as tenets of "success" simply because they work in the secular world.

Here are a few questions I hope will surface indirectly as we go forward from here:

1) Are churches that have a strong emphasis on business principles in danger of becoming the mainline traditional churches of the next millennium?

2) In churches that use business principles for evangelism are the percentages of people being baptized in water, filled with the Holy Spirit, and experiencing life-changing decisions increasing or decreasing compared to their denominational counterparts?

3) Are the "power signs" of Jesus' presence (i.e., healing, prophecy, demonic deliverance, etc.) increasing or decreasing in business principled churches?

4) Is the apparent increase in pastoral burnout related to the infusion of business principles into the church?

Of course, my hope is that many other questions will occur to the reader based on his/her background and present experience. If so, then the purpose of this paper will have occurred and people will have been stimulated to wrestle with the issue. So, here it goes.

WHAT I AM NOT SAYING

First of all, please allow me to define what I am NOT planning to say through the suggestions and questions of this article. I am NOT saying that all secular businesses or business principles are intrinsically evil, and therefore to be avoided at all costs. Neither am I saying that ANY inclusion of business concepts is automatically an EXCLUSION of God or godly principles. Finally, I am NOT saying that all successful kingdom ventures associated with business principles are a deception or unworthy of honest recognition.

It is not my desire to endict any church, organization, or individual as if I were in some judge's seat. I do not pretend to understand every facet of the relationship between the church and the business world, let alone the church and her Lord. Therefore, I am asking that the reader not assume that the information to follow is my attempt to root out what I see as an evil in the church, but rather an honest concern about where the church is headed as she prepares for a great final ingathering of souls and awaits the imminent return of Jesus the Lord.

OBSERVATIONS OF BUSINESS INFUSION
INTO THE CHURCH

Having completed my disclaimers, let me begin with some observations of what I consider to be introductions of business principles into the church.

Let's begin with church leadership styles and methods. According to Robert Logan, a nationally recognized consultant to churches (wonder where the term "consultant" came from), Apple CEO John Sculley and author Tom Peters have much to teach us about effective leadership. They are quoted as experts in Logan's book, "Beyond Church Growth".

I wonder about the effect of using models like Sculley and Peters on young, impressionable Pastors who are still groping their way out of seminary textbooks and into their own identities as men of God. In the short two decades or so since business principles have been openly espoused in the church I believe I have observed a radical shift in modeling from the strong, virile take charge CEO to the open, listening, inclusive leader of the 90's. It seems to me that many of the church leaders who bought into the 80's version of secular leadership became dictatorial and sometimes even arrogant in their discipling of others. Lording over people, demanding excellence from subordinates was acceptable because it was proven to be successful in business circles. Now, we've almost reached the other end of the pendulum, where inclusiveness is beginning to breed a "religiously correct" vernacular in the church.

My point is: depending on which decade you began to buy into business principles as an effective model for church leadership, that's what determined the kind of style you would lead with. And, that style may NOT agree with the Jesus' style or historically valued biblical precepts. My concern is where that is true do we depart from truth to become culturally relevant and chase the successful model?

Church leadership styles vary as greatly, of course. And, if we define "success" in terms of numbers of people who attend a church on Sunday mornings, we can legitimately say that every style has its champion. The question is, how has the infusion of business principles and models into the church affected leadership in general in the church? By the sheer volume of reading material on popular ministerial reading lists, relating to the business world one would have to say that at least the THINKING of the church has been greatly influenced. At the same time, through personal observation and informal surveys, I believe I can safely say that models of leadership based on business principles have burgeoned in the church.   So, I would suggest that the METHODOLOGIES of the church have also been greatly impacted.

EXAMPLES OF BUSINESS IMPACT ON THE CHURCH

One very obvious example of how the business world has influenced the church is the issue of marketing. Traditionally, evangelism methods have come predominantly through the inspiration of the Holy Spirit working through cutting edge leaders WITHIN the church. During the last decade, ideas about evangelism have come often from outside the church, things like marketing. Consequently, much of the church, in its quest to become "all things to all men", has become market driven and consumer oriented. Again, let me reiterate that I am NOT declaring what I see to be automatically evil or deceptive. I'm simply questioning where these changes will ultimately lead us.

Another example of business impact involves the terminology used in the cultural language of the church. Pastors have often, in the last decade, been compared or referred to as "CEO's". Terms like "infrastructure", "flow chart", "model" and others are now common place in the lingo of the church. These are all terms borrowed from the business world. Again, at the risk of redundancy, the question is NOT simply are these terms wrong in and of themselves, but how does the USE of them influence the thinking and actions of church leaders and congregations over the long haul?

Many of the new technological innovations being used by the church are also being directly transferred from the business world. Things like training videos, periodicals clearly modeled after worldly counterparts, telemarketing strategies, interior decorating techniques, are just of few examples of that.

WHEN, WHERE, AND WHY

The overriding issue is how, when, where, and why did business principles become so important to the church. Unfortunately, I cannot offer any concrete evidence on any of these questions. Documentation on the subject is hard to find because it has not been a significantly researched issue.

However, I can offer some suggestions that I think are worth consideration. These suggestions are not exclusively from my own contemplation but a conglomeration of conversations with many leaders in the church over a period of approximately one year.

How and when business principles were introduced in mass into the church I'm persuaded involves a long, slow process. Actually, as far back as the reign of Emperor Constantine, the church has assimilated business principles into the church. Consequently, I think there has always been a certain amount of influence exerted on the church by world institutions. However, for the purpose of this article (dealing with the church as it stands now) it is probably safe to say that the church opened wide to business principles sometime in the last 15-20 years primarily through the so-called "mega-church".

Possibly, the scenario goes something like this: as mega-churches began to grow their accounting and management procedures required some standards and methods not yet existing in the church at large. As those standards and methods were assimilated without repercussion the assumption was made (though probably not consciously) that other things could be assimilated also. This could be related to everything from the dramatic increase in the average salary of a Pastor over the last twenty years to the decrease in the length of an average Sunday morning service.

As to WHY the church opened up the welcome mat to business principles, I think the answer is complex with many facets. One possibility is that as the church (especially the Charismatic branch) went through the post Jesus/Charismatic movement lull, it was reaching for answers in the absence of a genuine move of God. Another potential answer lies in the success of the afore mentioned movements. As Spirit-filled life became more acceptable in the traditional denominations and our society in general it could be that success bred a new view of success into the church. Whereas the church had previously seen the transformation of souls as success it may possibly have been swayed into seeing success as a more numerical equation.

PROS AND CONS

Let me reiterate. I do NOT think that all use of business principles in the church is evil or suspect. In fact, especially when those principles reflect or support biblical truths, ideas transferred from the business world often come in a refreshing package.

The fact is, it is often the heart of the user that is the differential. In other words, many of the precepts used from the business community are neutral in their impact. Things like demographic studies, accounting principles, etc. can be useful or destructive depending on the user's bent.

Willow Creek Community Church outside of Chicago is a good example of a church that seems to be using a significant amount of business terminology as well as methodologies without losing their equilibrium.

However, Willow Creek may turn out to be the exception to the rule in the end. As one who has been in a supervisorial role of other churches and Pastors, I can say with a certain measure of confidence that there are not a few pastors and churches who have lost something of spiritual power with the advent of business expertise. It may seem judgmental, but I'm persuaded that it's an accurate assessment to say that many churches are at least in danger of substituting business principles for a personal relationship of communication and obedience to God.

Consider the following list of pros and cons concerning the subject at hand:

BUSINESS PROS	BUSINESS CONS
Often provide old truths in new packages (wineskins)	Packaging can be confused for quality substance
Accounting methods and other practical tools can make administration more effective	Can deceive people into thinking methods are the answer to all problems
Marketing and demographics can bring increased harvest	Methods can replace prayer as the supposed key to successful evangelism
Up-to-date business terms can make conversations with non-believers more relevant	Some business terms skew the truths attempting to be presented
Consumer-oriented approaches have proven to be successful in reaching this generation	If not followed up well, consumer-orientation can produce Christians who don't "take up their cross"

Obviously, the above list is abbreviated. However, there is enough there to understand the point, which is — business can be used in a positive or negative way depending on the internal inclination of the user.

WHAT THE BIBLE HAS TO SAY

It is an accepted fact among evangelical Christians that the arbiter of truth is the Bible, or the Word of God. So, let's take a quick look at a couple of passages which apply to our inquiry.

One of the classic verses used to affirm the use of business principle in the church is I Cor. 9:22:

> "I have become all things to all men so that by all possible means I might save some."

Most often when this text is used, the underlying thought is that if something is NOT in conflict with truths related to the kerygma of theology, or the user's personal convictions, then virtually any method or "means" of ministering to people is acceptable. And, I would agree. I think that much of what has been purported to be kerygma is actually nothing more that cultural wineskin. And, in those cases it is actually important to do something "different" so that people do not mistake substance for style.

In the first two chapters of the same book (I Cor.) there are several phrases that speak to the other side of the issue: "the foolishness of God is wiser than man's wisdom", "...not with words of human wisdom, lest the cross of Christ be emptied of its power", "God chose the weak things of the world to shame the strong", and "...not with wise and persuasive words, but with a demonstration of the Spirit's power".

The crux of what I hear Paul saying to the Corinthians, who were enamored with the world around them, was to beware of the inherent danger in trying to impress or finesse people into the kingdom...because in their attempts to be relevant to the world they MAY lose the very supernatural power of the gospel as intended by God. It's a difficult issue to discern, for sure, but one that cannot be ignored. Paul could not ignore it twenty centuries ago, and we cannot ignore it now.

One other important passage that pertains to our topic comes from the gospel of Luke and involves what I call the "spiritual two point reversal" (that's wrestling terminology describing when the person on the bottom is able to reverse positions through a particular move). Jesus put it this way:

> "...those who exercise authority over them (the Gentiles) call themselves Benefactors. But you are not to be like that.

Instead, the greatest among you should be like... one who serves."

As I have already alluded earlier in this paper, in the business world there are often styles of leadership espoused which call for a dictatorial kind of management. I've heard terminology like, "he got in my face" to describe "strong" leadership. And, I think that may speak more of business management than church leadership, at least as Jesus described it (and modeled it by washing their feet) in the above text.

A FEW SUMMARY STATEMENTS

So, what am I saying? Well, in simple form I hope this small paper has been a launching pad for further discussions by pressing the reader to: 1) ask the right questions about how the business world may be influencing their walk with Christ, their motivations for living, and their effectiveness in reaching the lost, 2) make any business principles transferred into the church fit into the context of scripture instead of the reverse, 3) examine the already acceptable business practices used by the church to discover their long term implications, and 4) challenge my assessments in conversations with other trusted Christians in order to learn through the collective wisdom and experience of those in the midst of the wrestling match.

I would also like to offer a few of my own observations which you may have picked up on in reading through this paper: 1) I AM deeply concerned about the long term implications of the influence of business principle in the church. I am persuaded by personal and observational experience that many pastors are being dissuaded from their real source of power, inspiration, and wisdom by taking the "easy way out" through desperate searches for those things in endless conferences, prolific periodicals, and oh-so-available videos. 2) I have a conviction that where business principles have overrun the church, those churches are in danger of becoming the mainline traditional churches of the next century, "having a form of godliness but denying the power thereof". 3) I am distressed by the numbers of pastors I see using business styles of leadership as a substitute for biblical mandates. I see too many young pastors, especially, looking more to secular models than biblical ones. And, I think the fallout in terms of how people in the congregation are being treated is going to have more impact than we can foresee in the immediate future.

I could go on, but I think you get the point. My prayer is that the Holy Spirit will help us, as only He can, to cut through the maze of debate and accurately delineate between the healthy use of business principles and the insidious assimilation of worldly thoughts and ideas. My desire is to be one used by God to influence young men to "ask for the ancient paths" and avoid the current pitfalls, where appropriate. Things like sacrifice and service must replace consumerism and "young buck" ladder climbing if the church is really going to be the agent for God's presence as we approach the 21st century. May the Lord of the church help us to see the difference and do something about it.

SELF-DIFFERENTIATION
Finding Your True Voice

Sam Rockwell

Pastoral authority is like a heavy-duty power tool. In skillful hands it can make one more efficient and more fruitful, but misused by the inept it can prove extremely hazardous or even deadly. To lead our churches effectively demands that we be neither heavy-handed in overusing our power nor wishy-washy through fear of using it at all. A balanced approach to spiritual authority pivots on our ability as leaders to define ourselves clearly and to take unambiguously defined positions in the face of confusion and resistance. Church life, as we all know from costly experience, abounds with conflicts centering around this issue.

For instance, every experienced pastor I have ever met has his own tale of a 'Jezebel' encounter. We all know how it gets started. Someone in the congregation begins to challenge the direction the church is going or to question the pastor's credibility by subtle comments (I sure hope the pastor is hearing the Lord on this), empathetic 'understanding' (I'm sure pastor means to be sensitive to our feelings), or superior spiritual insight (The Lord spoke to me and told me . . . .) It is amusing to catalogue the number of places where leaders have declared their particular geographical location a haven for the 'Jezebel spirit.' The problem arises from two factors: the invasiveness of a strong personality from the congregation and the commensurate passivity or 'tolerance' of the pastor [cf Revelation 2:20[1]]. Both conditions must be present for a 'Jezebel' situation to develop and cause damage.

Just as common, though, are the myriad of horror stories from laymen–those who still attend church, those who drift from this church to that, or those who have given up on churches altogether–of the brow-beating, domineering pastor whose control over his flock is absolute. These tales run amazingly parallel to one another as do the 'Jezebel' chronicles. There is no denying, of course, that there exist pastors who are so insensitive to others and so insecure in themselves that their control of everything that occurs in the church may not be questioned. This problem too thrives only under dual conditions: the passivity and dependence of the followers and the concomitant overpowering personality of the leader.

I am convinced that both these common church diseases can be cured—or avoided altogether. The answer lies in a reorientation of the pastor himself. An effective leader must steer carefully between the Scylla of "The true church consists of its parishioners and I am but their servant" and the Charybdis of "This is my church and I must govern it." Rather, a pastor must learn to lead from a deep sense of who he is and where he is headed as a person.

Edwin Friedman, in his book, *Generation to Generation: Family Process in Church and Synagogue*, writes about the importance of a spiritual leader's 'self-differentiation.' 'Differentiation' means the capacity to become oneself out of one's self with minimum reactivity to the positions or reactivity of others. 'Differentiation' is charting one's own way by means of one's own internal guidance system, rather than perpetually eyeing the 'scope' to see where others are.

> 'Differentiation' refers more to a process than to a goal that can ever be achieved. (To say, "I 'differentiated' from my wife, my child, my parent," etc., proves that the speaker does not understand the concept.) It refers to a direction in life rather than a state of being, to the capacity to take a stand in an intense emotional system, to saying 'I' when others are demanding 'we,' to containing one's reactivity to the activity of others (which includes the ability to avoid being polarized), to maintaining a non-anxious presence in the face of anxious others. It refers, as well, to knowing where one ends and another begins, to being able to cease automatically being one of the system's emotional dominoes, to being clear about one's own personal values and goals, to taking maximum responsibility for one's own emotional being and destiny rather than blaming others or the context: culture, gender, or environmental forces. It is an emotional concept, not a cerebral one, but it does require clearheadedness. And it has enormous consequence for new ways of thinking about leadership. But it is a lifetime project with no one ever getting more than seventy percent of the way to the goal.
>
> 'Differentiation' is not to be equated, however, with similar-sounding ideas such as individuation, autonomy, or independence. First of all, it has less to do with a person's behavior than, as mentioned, with his or her emotional being.

Second, there is a sense of connectedness to the concept that prevents the mere gaining of distance or leaving, no less cutting off, from being the way to achieve it. Third, as stated above, it has to do with the fabric of one's existence, one's integrity.[2]

A pastor's leadership, then, must become a natural, organic function of the direction in which his life is already heading, of his own 'differentiation,' if you will. Otherwise, he will always be susceptible to the disastrous scenarios already described. We pastors risk forfeiting our leadership any time we placate intimidating and intransigent people who covertly undermine us as we naively stand by, or we fail to deal with them swiftly because we fear a backlash or because we are privately unsure of ourselves and our position. On the other hand, we cannot afford to become intimidating and intransigent ourselves, pushing or pulling others along instead of leading them with a clear, strong voice.

The dilemmas we face when attempting to navigate the shoals of evaluating and shaping our roles as power-brokers are several fold. We desire to lead decisively and confidently, exercising personal initiative and a strong sense of stewardship concerning our responsibilities. Concurrently, we wish to relinquish control to God, to exhibit submission, humility and magnanimity toward our following. We may mistake weakness and passivity in ourselves for submission to God and others.[3] After all, submission is a passive stance to some degree. Similarly, we may mistake our own bull-headedness for commitment. The answer is not in attempting to strike a balance between these poles as much as it is to see a third alternative altogether–leadership through *self-differentiation*.

Scratching my head one afternoon over these bipolar issues, I constructed a quadrant diagram. The horizontal axis is a continuum (from 0 to 100) representing congregational growth into commitment and initiative. The vertical axis is a continuum (from 0 to 100) representing congregational growth into submission and humility. The stick figures in each quadrant reflect whether or not the factor of submission and commitment are proportional to one another and, most importantly, how the functioning of the pastor (represented by the stick head!) affects the 'body' or his followers. The diagram is meant to emphasize continuity and process rather than discrete categories. (The quadrants are not presented in numerical order.)

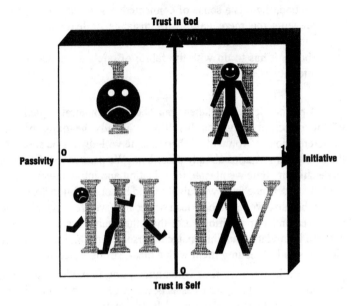

QUADRANT I: THE BODILESS HEAD

This quadrant is characterized by a strong, perhaps angry, self-styled leader who is demanding and overly aggressive. The congregational 'body' of such a 'head' may prosper in times of duress or when the people are particularly in need of safety and security, and to remain intact they may need a 'cause' or something/someone to oppose. A potential danger here is the development of a Cult, which breeds on the militaristic, oppositional characteristics of a personality-based leader. The 'bodiless head' creates by definition a climate where the pastor must over-function to survive, while his parishioners, often docile and detached from genuine participation, are only too happy to abdicate all responsibility to him. And he is happy to take it—until he burns out. An over-functioning pastor tends to create clones rather than disciples.

This congregation exists on the high end of the submission continuum, but there is minimum corresponding action or initiative on its part and therefore not a genuine submission being expressed. A passive church does not create a dominant pastor, however. On the contrary, the reverse is true.

QUADRANT IV: THE HEADLESS BODY

In this scenario the distinctiveness of the pastor–his leadership style, his philosophy of ministry, his vision—may create uneasiness and suspicion in members who themselves wield power in the congregation. A 'body' of this type may be manipulated by a person or group of persons who are well-entrenched and have a strong sense of ownership over the church's agenda. Any hesitancy on the part of the pastor will inevitably cause strong lay personalities to become inflamed in their opposition to focused leadership. This kind of 'body,' where commitment to the emotional safety of the group is valued more than change and growth, is especially susceptible to the Jezebel problem and will, in general, tend to be less innovative and less likely to take risks. Because peace and togetherness are primary values in this 'body,' an obstinate follower is often allowed too much leverage. (If 'peace' is the primary value of your family, for instance, you may forego previously laid plans for the evening in deference to your screaming three-year-old.) Peace at the high price of progress may be the cost of group 'headless body' leadership.

This congregation sits on the high end of the initiative continuum but low on the submission axis. Again, it is important to note that the weakness of the leader creates the necessary conditions for weakness in the congregation and not vice versa. Weak fathers breed spoiled children, not the other way round. A pastor may inherit a quadrant IV or a quadrant I church, but his consistent, well-differentiated leadership will ultimately result in healthier, functioning people.

QUADRANT III: A COMPLETE WASHOUT

Not too many churches remain viable when there is neither submission to God nor personal ommitment. Most quadrant III-type churches will eventually take on the characteristics of either quadrants I, II or IV because a vacuum, as represented by this quadrant, begs to be filled—either by a health-inducing agent (a quadrant II leader) or a pathogenic one (a quadrant I or IV leader).

QUADRANT II:
THE BODY WITH A GOOD HEAD ON ITS SHOULDERS

This 'body' enjoys a leader who is well-positioned, one who is at once deeply connected to his people through mutual submission and yet differentiated from them by his own personal commitment. Our endeavor to be well-positioned calls for us to be engaged in two painful and soul-searching processes:

1. the quest to discover how our church is related to our own uniqueness as individuals, and

2. the imperative of dealing with sabotage to the above process.

The idea that our ministry is to some degree an extension of our individuality may seem at first to be narcissistic. On closer examination, however, we can see that it is not. The Apostle Paul, uniquely prepared by personality, history, education, and revelation to be the torch-bearer to the Gentiles, could ill-afford to compare himself to the other apostles. His call was intensely personal and custom fit.

> *For I would have you know, brethren, that the gospel which was preached by me is not according to man. For I neither received it from man, nor was I taught it, but I received it through a revelation of Jesus Christ. For you have heard of my former manner of life in Judaism, how I used to persecute the church of God beyond measure and tried to destroy it; and I was advancing in Judaism beyond many of my contemporaries among my countrymen, being more extremely zealous for my ancestral traditions. But when He who had set me apart, even from my mothers' womb, and called me through His grace was pleased to reveal His Son in me that I might preach Him among the Gentiles, I did not immediately consult with flesh and blood, nor did I go up to Jerusalem to those who were apostles before me; but I went away to Arabia, and returned once more to Damascus.*
>
> *Then three years later I went up to Jerusalem to become acquainted with Cephas and stayed with him fifteen days. But I did not see any other of the apostles except James, the Lord's brother.* Galatians 1:11-19

For Paul, to have focused on what seemed to work elsewhere would have spelled his certain failure. In his letter he posits a number of considerations that, in his eyes, give credibility to himself and his ministry. First, his ministry is a result of a personal encounter with Christ, a product not of second-hand knowledge but of first-hand experience. Second, the Apostle's ministry is grounded on the idea that it is unique, that both he and it have been set apart. Third, Paul glories in the fact that neither he nor his ministry has been diluted by undue peer influence.

At some point and in some way in our ministerial lives, each of us must push away from the pack—the consultants, the idea-generators, the church-growth gurus, the 'successful models'—and find out for ourselves who we are: to what specifically have I been called? how am I unique? what inherent qualities of leadership do I possess? As it was with both Paul and Jesus, perhaps the specter of personal failure or some other kind of wilderness experience is the petri dish for this kind of self discovery. To become an originator instead of merely an imitator takes great courage, long-term durability, and emotional maturity. By 'originator,' I do not necessarily mean one whose structures, approaches or ideas are particularly novel or radically different, but one out of whose call, gifting and vision these things appear—or are conceived—as natural by-products.[4]

What am I called to create? Is the ministry I'm developing one that I would readily participate in if I were a layman? An outsider? On our present course, will I love this church in ten years? Am I on an endless quest for new methods? Is this search an indication of my own lack of direction and conviction?

When a pastor can take a clear, specific stand based on the process of working out his own salvation, he has no need to 'motivate' others. He has no need to cajole, incite, placate or appease. He simply goes to where he is going. The steady posture and pace of a confident leader create their own attraction, their own following. I believe sure-footedness, while making us less vulnerable to overbearing people interested only in their own agenda, is also more apt to engender followers who discover their own niche in the scheme of things. Both pathogens of passivity and stubborn self-will are given less fuel to feed on when the leader is cohesive in his thinking and consistent in his actions.

Opposition is inevitable though. Resistance may come not only because there is disagreement about our ideas or vision but because we dare to lead at all. Especially if we have been too non-committal or have sounded an uncertain trumpet. Those in the congregation who are most pastor-dependent will experience the most anxiety about their leaders 'pull-out.' For example, followers may instinctively respond to the loss of control they experience due to a reassertion of direction by their leader.[5] When a pastor seeks to move his 'body' from quadrant IV to quadrant II, his followers may feel like he is moving to quadrant I. He may be very tempted to maintain the status quo as the prospect of conflict becomes more imminent.

For some followers, the predictability of their leader is a source of great emotional comfort, and his personal renewal may therefore threaten them deeply, probably on a level they cannot articulate. Almost certainly the emotional tension will manifest itself in some 'issue.' It behooves the pastor at such times to be wise enough to see through the 'issue' to the real problem: the knee-jerk emotional reaction of overly-dependent followers. A leader must take a stand of quiet confidence and resist getting drawn into a war of wills. It is very difficult for any leader to create a challenging situation when he knows full well that to do so will stir up misunderstanding and adversity. This, however, is a test of leadership. Am I willing to allow the more dependent members of my church to experience pain? Can I handle their rejection if it comes to that? Just as we, the leaders, must be willing to walk through the wilderness of submission, loss of and eventual re-discovery of self, so must our followers. If we cannot bear to see our followers experience the pain of wilderness, we will cease to really lead them. If we fail to allow and sometimes even to precipitate pain in our followers, we become mere hirelings, therapeutic hand-holders, and not true shepherds.

It is easy for a pastor to protect his members from pain and subsequent growth by failing to direct them specifically or to make his position unwaveringly clear. As he senses disgruntlement and resentment of followers whom he challenges, it is vital for him to maintain his position without being defensive, combative, or emotionally coercive. The quality of one's character when in the throes of conflict will ultimately determine his strength to lead when the dust settles.

Personal growth as a leader seems to come at the high price of having to determine what is ultimately important at crucial crossroads. Will we endure short term upheaval for the sake of long term fruitfulness? Can we stand up under the pain of confronting unpleasant realities, knowing very well we will disrupt the 'peace' and our false sense of security? The real challenge is not so much the prospect of confronting overbearing individuals as much as the trepidation of facing our fears and insecurities.

Becoming a well-positioned leader is about searching out for ourselves what we believe about church life and acting decisively on our convictions. When we seek to dominate because we are not really sure of ourselves or equivocate because we are not really sure of ourselves, we keep our churches in a state of perpetual infancy. And the only way to grow up is to lead ourselves and our people through an acute and painful process of change.

As we all know, one of the factors that contribute to the gawkiness and lack of coordination in adolescents is that they are passing through puberty. Growing up as a leader is also a process of gaining strength in our muscles, giving our brains and emotions time to catch up with our lengthening limbs and to become familiar with and attuned to our own bodies. Perhaps, when the cracks and squeaks have all been worked out of our developing vocal chords, we will one day discover that we have come to recognize the sound of our own voice.

NOTES

1. Revelation 2:20 *But I have this against you, that you tolerate the woman Jezebel, who calls herself a prophetess, and she teaches and leads My bond-servants astray, so that they commit acts of immorality and eat things sacrificed to idols.*

2. Edwin Friedman, *Generation to Generation: Family Process in Church and Synagogue*, (Guilford Press, 1985), pp 228-234. The primary thesis of this book is that each clergyman, regardless of faith, is simultaneously involved in three distinct families: the families within his congregation, his congregation itself, and his own family. "Because the emotional process in all of these systems is identical, unresolved issues in any one of them can produce symptoms in the others, and increased understanding of any one creates more effective functioning in all three." This book is helpful in making sense of the emotional dynamics involved in leading people during conflict.

3. I recently revisited *Spiritual Authority*, the classic by Watchman Nee, which includes an insightful explication of the issues of spiritual authority and submission, discussing the responsibilities of both the leader and the follower. "All who hearken to God's direct authority but reject delegated authority are nonetheless under the principle of rebellion . . . Authority being the most central thing in the whole Bible, reviling against it constitutes the gravest sin." Nee makes the point that one who rebels against authority is one who is not subjecting himself to God, though it may appear to the rebel that he is rejecting some impure manifestation of God's authority through a human channel. For a leader, Nee suggests two characteristics of an authority who is walking in genuine submission himself. First, he does not listen to scandalous words. "Those who are disturbed and overwhelmed by words of slander prove themselves unfit to be a delegated authority." Second, a leader must not defend himself. "Authority and self-defense are incompatible. The one against whom you defend yourself becomes your judge. Whenever one tries to justify himself, he loses authority."

4. In *Creating Minds: An Anatomy of Creativity Seen Through the Lives of Freud, Einstein, Picasso, et. al.*, (Harper Collins, 1993), Howard Gardner argues that the 'creators' in his book made their contributions to their disciplines after roughly ten years of tireless dedication to mastering them, combined with the courage and brilliance to challenge them. Could there be a lesson for us here? Is it possible that imitation precedes originality? 'Pushing away from the pack' may be foolish for the naive or the young inexperienced pastor. Never to 'push away' in some way or another, however, would certainly be a pity. Indeed, Gardner observes, "it would be unwarranted to contend that one first follows the craft for ten years and one

then strikes out on one's own . . . Individuals who ultimately make creative breakthroughs tend from the earliest days to be explorers, innovators, tinkerers."

5. In *The Making of a Leader*, (NavPress, 1988), Robert Clinton discusses 'leadership backlash.' The "leadership backlash process item refers to the negative reaction of followers, other leaders within the group, and Christians outside the group to a course of action taken by a leader once ramifications develop from the decision." He sets forth this pattern:

1. The leader gets a vision (direction) from God.

2. The followers are convinced of the direction.

3. The group moves in the direction given.

4. The group experiences persecution, hard times, or attacks from Satan. Spiritual warfare is common.

5. There is backlash from the group.

6. The leader is driven to God to seek affirmation in spite of the action's ramifications.

7. God reveals Himself further—who He is, what He intends to do. He makes it clear that He will deliver.

8. God vindicates Himself and the leader.

LOOKING BEYOND THE OBVIOUS
An Introduction to Systems Thinking

David Sather

There was a man in the construction industry that had the reputation of a professional fixer. He could go to any job requiring patchwork and leave knowing that no one could do a finer job. He was in every sense of the term a craftsman with a putty knife. From commercial to residential, from the poshest of hotels to the average home, this man would come and repair holes in walls, making cracks disappear. His reputation grew and people within the community began to rely on him to patch everything. The money was good, he enjoyed the attention, and soon almost every structure within the community had been at one time or another touched by his handiwork.

As his reputation grew, so did the expectations. While he used to be called only for small repair work, which he was trained to do, now he was called for everything. Holes in walls became stress fractures in foundations. Little cracks in plaster became questions about the structural integrity of a building. Yet he plunged ahead. The problems began shortly after earthquake hit. An expert at surface repairs, he did not know how to respond to the fact that when strain was placed on the structures he had patched, the surface patches could not withstand the strain. The quick fixes that had impressed so many people, that looked so good on the outside, were now gaping holes. All those years of work did not last.

Much like the craftsman so adept at patching holes and fixing cracks, pastors and church leaders have become accustomed and, in fact, highly specialized in the area of the quick fix. If a problem arises within the church, the Pastor is called to fix it. As long as we do a job well enough that it is not visible on the outside, people are satisfied. The problem with the quick fixes churches have grown accustomed to is the same problem the craftsman ran into. The moment stress is added to the structure the cracks reappear, and previously satisfied customers (or loyal followers) become disgruntled and demand better workmanship.

This paper will introduce a concept called Systems Thinking. "A system is a perceived whole whose elements 'hang together' because they continuously affect each other over time and operate toward a common purpose."[1]   Systems Thinking is "a framework for seeing inter-relationships rather than things; to see the forest in the trees."[2]   If ever there was a perceived whole whose elements affect each other over time, it is the church.

Paul tells us in Romans 12:4-5 *"For as we have many members in one body, but all the members do not have the same function, so we, being many, are one body in Christ, and individually members of one another."* There has always been an interdependency within the local church. We are taught to rely on one another, to utilize our strengths and bolster our weaknesses. The church is compared numerous times in Scripture to the human body. Each part, each division works together toward a common purpose. Systems thinking reintroduces this idea. The church was intended to be led as a whole organism, not through fragmenting it into parts. Each part of the body affects another. Any decision made will create ripples throughout the whole structure.

This paper will not attempt to offer answers to the dilemmas facing today's leadership, rather it is my hope that this paper will cause the reader to ask intelligent questions. It will not offer solutions to specific problems, but rather will open up an opportunity to develop the ability to look beyond the obvious fix. Many times the problems we face today are the result of choices we made in years past.

Whether we pastor large churches with staff full-time or have to work a second job and pastor part-time, the man in the cartoon could be any one of us. We have all faced at one time or another problems and challenges. Each dilemma, each challenge, represents a barrier to what we hope for our church. Birthed out of the desire to survive the next year, our tendency is to deal with them as quickly and as painlessly as possible. So we embark on our own form of crisis management. We study, we ponder, we prayerfully consider the problem staring us in the face, then we handle it as best we can. Because the problems are so familiar, the solutions are too. Management crises are addressed the same as they were 10 years ago. "Businesses and corporations in trouble almost always respond to crisis by doing more of what they have already done."[3] The focus is on changing what the root causes **produce** rather than the root causes themselves.[4] We become reactive in our problem solving, addressing the obvious — the squeaky wheel — while forgetting about the axle about to fail. In the process we do not realize that our solution, however well intentioned, does not take into consideration the rest of the system. The fix that was supposed to be the simplest, least painful, generates a ripple that affects the whole community. The solution too many times creates another set of issues which need to be addressed, or ran from — depending upon who's derriere's in the chair.

Whether out of necessity or environment, we have adopted a western view of management in assuming that the parts are primary. We have divided what is described scripturally as a living, breathing organism into pieces and parts. Instead of legs and arms we label them midweek meetings, children's programs, self-help programs, youth groups, and worship teams. These divisions, rather than being seen as parts of a whole that function together toward a common goal, are too often treated separately. Instead, structures are set up which allow parts to flourish and function completely independent of the whole. Leading the church by dividing the body into parts has robbed us of one of our primary tools — viewing the organization as an interconnected system. Decisions too often are made with only pieces of information coming from fragmented parts of the body. The structure no longer provides the leader with the whole picture. We implement changes that address only surface issues because we do not see the "Big Picture" or the "System". One idea of Systems Thinking is recognizing the ramifications and tradeoffs of the actions we choose.

Let me relate this idea to a concept we are all familiar with, implementing small groups in the local church. My purpose is not to debate the pros or cons of such a move, only to point out a dilemma when implementing such a change. In his book <u>Prepare your Church for the Future</u>, Carl George compares cell growth with yeast.

Too many church growth ideas are quick fixes; they offer cosmetic changes to the system. They "patch cracks." The change is noticeable; the growth at times is rapid. But rarely do cosmetic changes alter the structure. Small groups do not provide only external changes, but rather can cause the church to undergo a systemic change over a period of time. Church can become participatory. People meeting in homes, meeting needs without the professional pastor in charge. It pushes people into an active role in ministry. It offers growth through relationships, not relying solely on Sunday morning. For the pastor who acknowledges the built-in delay factor, and prepares for it, this can be a healthy move. But to the one who is used to dealing with "quick fixes," small groups are a frightening endeavor, and are usually abandoned within the first year.

The following diagram illustrates the same principle systemically.

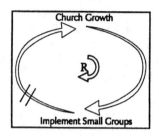

This diagram is a reinforcing feedback loop. "A reinforcing feedback loop compounds change with even more change. It is responsible for rapid growth, such as the proliferation of cells in a test tube or the accumulation of money in a savings account. Frequently reinforcing loops are called positive feedback loops, vicious or virtuous cycles, snowball effect, or band wagon effect."[5] The goal is stated on top — **Church Growth**. The bottom heading offers a solution — **The Implementation of Small Groups**. The arrows indicate that as a church grows more small groups will be formed, creating more growth, creating more small groups, creating more growth — a reinforcing cycle. On the surface it appears to offer a quick and painless way to grow. How hard can small groups be? We find five volunteers who can teach; we build it up on five consecutive Sunday mornings, and the people are excited. A month down the road this looks like the ideal thing. Finally we have stumbled onto something that actually works. However, a year later two groups die; two others need to be euthanized, and this leaves the Pastor with only one. Why didn't it work out? It appears to be a total failure. So we abandon it, and search out the bookstore for another idea, only one that works this time.

In this scenario the Pastor has done what he has been taught to do. He should look for and expect results immediately. In doing so, he fails to look upon the endeavor systemically. He forgets about the time delay. In the above diagram, the two lines dissecting the left arrows indicates this delay. There can be a time delay of five to ten years for small groups to affect the structure. (Structure is "the pattern of interrelationships among key components of the system."[6]) Looking at the picture systemically shows the pastor his options and possible difficulties he will face.

A much more common scenario is found in the pastor who desires to see his church grow spiritually. He begins to look for leaders with experience — the **"MATURE ONES."** Below is a very simple causal loop diagram illustrating this point.

The pastor looks for the most qualified, mature people in his church to lead the people to spiritual growth. The more qualified leaders he finds, the faster his church will mature. In his desire to see change happen fast, he finds the most willing participant.

In an ideal situation this diagram would never change. As we use the leadership, the church grows. As the church grows, more leadership becomes available — maturity, upon maturity, upon maturity. This is another example of a reinforcing feedback loop. Each action reinforces the other, resulting in a spiraling growth in experienced leadership and spirituality. Too many times, however, the choices have unintended consequences. Initially, the mature leadership does such a good job, the younger Christians stop volunteering. The situation worsens when the development of new leaders comes to a halt. We have created a balancing feedback loop. "Balancing feedback loops maintain balance. They try to negate change in one direction by pushing in the opposite direction. A thermostat, which regulates temperature in a house, or hunger, which regulate food consumption in the human body, are both examples of balancing feedback loops. They are also frequently called negative feedback loops."[7]

The next diagram shows the consequences of a seemingly innocent decision. Too many times in our search for experienced leaders we neglect a greater resource — people with no experience but a willingness to try. Our choice creates a reinforcing feedback loop that eventually diminishes spiritual growth not increases it.

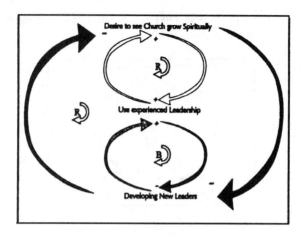

Here the frustration begins. What am I to do? If I do not use experienced leadership, then who will teach Sunday School? Who is going to lead worship? Then you tell me the answer to all my problems, if I am willing to wait it out, is small groups. Yes, I know you didn't say that but it was implied. These many questions are the beginning of looking at the organization systemically — trying to see the parts as related to the whole body, not separate. Asking questions helps us see beyond the surface of an issue.

We all have the tendency to look for results. We want to see the bottom line and we want it now. We are in a business that measures results as specifically as any corporation's profit and loss statement. The survival rate is gauged in terms of months on the job, not years. Therefore, it is natural to seek out answers to specific problems. It is also just as natural, when exposed to a group of ideas that offer more questions and no solutions to wonder why bother. Where does this fit in for me when I go back to my office and the Children's Director is screaming for more help? Or the Worship Leader just informed you that your drummer and lead guitarist got into a fight over artistic differences. Maybe it fits because it causes the leader to slow down and avoid reacting. It fits because it is a tool that can be used in the decision making process. It offers the user better eyesight. "Incorporating these tools into our daily life requires what David McCamus, former Chairman and CEO of Xerox Canada, calls 'peripheral vision': the ability to pay attention to the world as if through a wide-angle, not a telephoto lens, so you can see how your actions interrelate with other areas of activity."[8]

"Buckminster Fuller said that if you want to teach people a new way of thinking, don't bother trying to teach them. Instead, give them a tool, the use of which will lead to new ways of thinking."[9] I have worked on numerous construction sites in various capacities. While each site has different requirements there was always one common denominator—a hammer. This hammer would be used for a hundred different jobs, in a hundred different ways. It is used to build and to break apart. It is used as a wedge and a pry bar, a nail puller and something to throw when you hit your finger. Though I have purchased numerous hammers over the years, I never had one that came with an instruction manual. I took it to the job site and used it anyway I could.

I cannot hope to teach, but I can offer a new tool. This tool is called "Systems Thinking". Use it as you will. Grow accustomed to the feel of it. Pull it off the shelf every once in awhile and swing it. I think you will find that it fits rather nicely in your collection. To paraphrase Albert Einstein, "Our present problems cannot be solved at the same level of thinking at which they were created." So swing away.

NOTES

1. Senge, Peter, The Fifth Discipline Fieldbook, Doubleday, New York, New York, pg. 90.

2. Kreutzer, David, Introduction to Systems Thinking, Gould-Kreutzer Associates, Inc., Cambridge, MA 02142.

3. Block, Peter, Stewardship, Berret-Koehler Publishers, San Francisco, 1993, pg. xv.

4. Argyris, Chris, Overcoming Organizational Defenses, Allyn and Bacon, Needham Heights, MA, 1990, pg. 4.

5. Kreutzer, et.al.

6. Senge, Peter, The Fifth Discipline Fieldbook, Doubleday, New York, New York, pg. 90.

7. Kreutzer, et.al.

8. Senge, et.al.

9. Ibid.

BIBLIOGRAPHY

Generation to Generation, Family Process in Church and Synagogue, Edwin H. Friedman, The Guilford Press, New York, 1985.

Introduction to Systems Thinking, David Kreutzer, Gould-Kreutzer Associates, Inc., Cambridge, MA 02142.

Overcoming Organizational Defenses, Chris Argyris, Allyn and Bacon, Needham Heights, MA, 1990.

Stewardship, Peter Block, Berret-Koehler Publishers, San Francisco, 1993.

The Fifth Discipline, The Art & Practice of the Learning Organization, Peter Senge, Doubleday, New York, New York, 1990.

The Fifth Discipline Fieldbook, Peter Senge, Art Kleiner, Charlotte Roberts, Richard Ross, and Bryan Smith, Doubleday, New York, New York

ATTITUDES FOR REVITALIZING A LOCAL CHURCH
Preliminary Attitudes Necessary In Becoming A Church Planting Congregation

John A. Tolle

INTRODUCTION

These are great days for the church of Jesus Christ! Millions of faithful, Jesus Christ-honoring believers fill the estimated 350,000-400,000 Protestant churches in the United States.(1) Yet, as many as 100,000 of these churches may close their doors in the next few years. America, once the premier "Christian" nation in the world, is today the largest English-speaking mission field in the world. Some reports suggest that more than 200 million people are non practicing Christians or have no relationship with Jesus Christ.(2) The decline of Christianity in North America does not paint a pretty picture nor give the church much hope, yet, I believe, these are great days for the church. This bleak assessment should awaken us.

On the positive side, the last 10-15 years have seen solid emphasis placed upon the starting of new churches to more effectively reach our nation and the world for Jesus Christ. Approximately 35,000 churches began during the decade of the 80's in the United States.(3) Many have suggested this to be the most effective means of advancing the Kingdom of God. Though this church planting accomplishment is noteworthy, it has not kept pace with population growth nor with the church closure rate. This has happened on the heels of two-decades-worth of teaching the Biblical principle of "the ministry of every believer." Many churches teach about releasing members into vital ministry, the starting of new churches, of spiritual renewal; but talking is not doing. Too few have caught Jesus' vision and mission for the church. His commission to the disciples (Matthew 28:18-20, Mark 16:15, Luke 24:47-48, Acts 1:8), held in the light of Matthew 16:16-18, spoke of a triumphing church. The aforementioned decline suggests that the "gates of hell" are hindering the church. Jesus' church should be more successful than it is. This picture may seem dismal but the future of Jesus' church need not be. These are great days for His church.

"Do you not say, 'There are still four months and then comes the harvest'? Behold, I say to you, lift up your eyes and look at the fields, for they are already white for harvest!"
(John 4:35)

We must make the choices to see the trend of spiritual decline reversed. More about that in a moment.

This modest proposal intends to provoke a reexamination of our concepts for church ministry. Nothing will be shockingly new or outlandish — just Biblical material worthy of reexamination. While many are blind to the current problem of church decline in America there are many who are wrestling with reaching a generation with the Gospel of Jesus Christ. As mentioned above, many individuals and churches have caught the vision of evangelization through church planting. But with the church closure rate being substantially higher than that of the number planted, it is imperative more enlist into the church planting ranks. Too few, it appears, are involved in such significant Kingdom extending enterprise. For that to take place, many traditional, established, and existing churches must be transformed and revitalized.

"The harvest truly is plentiful, but the laborers are few. Therefore, pray the Lord of the harvest to send out laborers into His harvest." (Matthew 9:37-38)

Such a call for transformation and revitalization is "the experiment in progress" at Living Word Christian Fellowship in Newbury Park, California. I will try to identify some major attitudinal adjustments needed to allow revitalization to occur. It is my belief that these adjustments must be made wherever a church is to become the scriptural entity that Jesus prescribed it to be.

CHURCH BACKGROUND

The church is in its twelfth year of existence and began more by accident than by plan. Within months of its inception it was apparent

God's hand was upon the church. Young adults with common goals and an excitement to do something significant for God were attracted to the vibrant "new" church meeting in the local park's community center. Joy and excitement characterized those early days. The church grew rapidly for several years, topped out, then began to decline. The decline nearly became disastrous. This condition required changes be made to set the ministry back on course. The founding pastor, after heroically weathering the storm and seeing stability restored, set out to birth a new congregation. That change brought my wife and me to the church.

After the founding pastor launched out to birth another congregation, it became apparent the church's vision was not one of church planting but that of survival. Such a state of affairs did not invalidate the former pastor's church planting effort but does reveal how the church perceives itself and its mission. Until the church regains a sense of its God-given purpose, its ministry, including evangelism and future church planting efforts, will remain good, but limited at best. The following comments regarding prayer, purposes, and attitudes are key factors in how we are addressing the issue of church revitalization.

THE ANSWER IS PRAYER

With the work of the church being spiritual in nature it makes sense that the elements needed to reverse the decline and bring revitalization must be spiritual (I Corinthians 2:9-14). Ultimately, the church's efforts will fail or it will suffer decline if spiritual revitalization does not occur. A refreshed working of the Holy Spirit is needed and the answer is a new call to prayer. Although worship, Bible studies, fellowship, etc. are all important functions necessary for spiritual growth, I am convinced that the revitalization of the church is only possible where pastor and people dedicate themselves to prayer. The presence of the Holy Spirit and the openness of the people to His working is crucially important.

Prayer has been the key to every revival in the history of Christianity. The disciples, before the Day of Pentecost, "were continually in the temple, praising and blessing God" "with one accord in prayer and supplication" (Luke 24:53, Acts 1:14). The church was born when the Holy Spirit descended during one of these times of concentrated prayer.

In the early stages of the church, the Holy Spirit gave revelation to the leaders gathered in Antioch that they should send Barnabas and Saul to perform missionary ministry, the planting of churches. Yet, the Holy Spirit only spoke after they had been in fasting and prayer (Acts 13, 14).

Martin Luther's dissatisfaction with the religious world of his time and his yearning for personal devotion to Christ led him to spend much time in prayer. During the winter of 1512 he locked himself in a room to pray. This time of earnest prayer and searching the scriptures ultimately resulted in the Reformation.(4/5)

As the revival fires began to diminish following the Reformation and the Age of Enlightenment (characterized by rationalism, skepticism, and a pagan concept of man's supreme worth) emerged, it was the prayer and fasting of men like John and Charles Wesley with George Whitefield that led to a worldwide revival that included the birth of Method-ism.(6)

Then, during the nineteenth century the church stumbled into "higher criticism." It was the anointed preaching, the result of continual prayer and fasting, of men like Charles Finney, Dwight L. Moody, and R.A. Torrey that God used to bring the breakthrough that helped usher in the Pentecostal movement of the early 1900's.(7)

In the 1960 and '70's it was prayer that ignited the Jesus People and Charismatic movements and it will be prayer . . . again, which will cause the revitalization of the church and an awakening to the world.

Two quotes from E.M. Bounds have recently refreshed my desire to place a priority upon prayer.(8)

> *"Prayer is the first thing, the second thing, the third thing necessary to a minister. Pray, then my dear brother; pray, pray, pray."* — Sir Thomas Buston
>
> *"No man can do a great and enduring work for God who is not a man of prayer, and no man can be a man of prayer who does not give much time to praying."*

THE CHURCH'S PURPOSE

As we, through prayer, recapture the heart of God for His church upon this earth, we need to seize a renewed understanding of His purposes for the church. Summarized below are four statements that apply to most churches.(9)

1. The church exists, first and foremost, to **exalt** God. Teaching believers, individually and corporately, to praise and worship God is our highest call.

2. The church exists to **edify** believers through teaching, fellowship, expressions of worship, prayer, and breaking of

bread. Believers must constantly be challenged to grow into full maturity in Christ.

3. The church exists to **extend** the heart of God to others through expressions of service. Each individual has a role to fulfill if the church is to be Christ's legitimate expression to the world.

4. The church exists to **expand** God's kingdom. God has instructed us to make Him known to the world through loving acts of evangelism and mission.

A basic commitment to these four foundational purposes will help maintain the church's balance and will cause its growth in quality and quantity.

OUR ATTITUDE

The following is the preliminary attitudinal strategy for seeing the church revitalized. Though many matters seem important (i.e., organizational structure, programs, budgets, facilities, etc.) it is my belief we must revolutionize our attitude for ministry by clarifying the following three things. We must:

1. Recapture Jesus' call for fruitful discipleship; fulfilling all that Jesus Christ intended discipleship to be when he commanded us to "go . . . make disciples."

2. Redefine the concept of ministry; returning to the basic truth that every member is a minister and that my pastoral ministry is to help equip people for their God-given ministries.

3. Renew My Attitude for Leadership Selection and Development; recognizing that Jesus' model seems radically different from most utilized today. He took risks with some we would call jerks.

1. Recapture Jesus' Call for Fruitful Discipleship

There are countless thousands of Christians all across America who make serving Jesus Christ their primary priority of life. Discipleship to them is studying and memorizing scripture, practicing a set of disciplines, etc. While this is noble and I might add, these practices should continue, we must accept that this methodology has not accomplished the goal of Jesus to "go and make disciples." I agree with what Jim Petersen says in "LIFESTYLE DISCIPLESHIP." "Thirty years of discipleship programs, and we are not discipled."(10) Discipleship, as such, has become regimented. It is generally a program that emphasizes the mastering of information, attempted life interaction with the information, and hopefully some means of recapitulating the information to another. These are elements of discipleship but consider that most discipleship occurs in 12 week courses or similar types of classes with only a limited time commitment. Life change, the real goal of discipleship does not take place so quickly. It requires a lifetime of responding to God and His purposes. Simply put, it requires pursuing God so that one becomes intimate with Him. As a result, transformation into Jesus' likeness occurs. See Ephesians 2:10 and 4:13.

Transformation is the key. Too often discipleship programs have required a few adjustments to include God in ones life, the changing of a few habits, and some semblance of participation in church life. I am suggesting that real discipleship requires radical life change. The need for brevity allows for only a synopsis of what I am suggesting.

This process of spiritual change begins with a supernatural transformation. It is at this point of conversion that the Holy Spirit moves into a person to become the primary change agent for the remainder of the individual's life. Some things change immediately and permanently at the time of this transaction while other matters take an entire lifetime. We also see how the kind of change we are dealing with is not merely behavior modification. It is not just stopping one set of practices to take on another. It focuses on the transformation of the person we are. From the inside out, Jesus Christ works His nature into our lives by changing our values, then our behavior.

2. Redefine the Concept of Ministry

For too long "the ministry" has referred to the activity of the professional clergy. Such reference terribly limits the term and impedes the development and growth of Jesus' church. If we are going to see the church extended into the world it will require that we more adequately release the people to minister the life of Jesus in very meaningful ways. Jesus Christ has given spiritual leaders the responsibility to develop every believer "for the work of the ministry" so that the church is edified (Ephesians 4:12). And it is interesting, God has constructed his church (the body of Christ) so that each member has a function and role to perform (Romans 12:3-8, I Corinthians 12:12-14, Ephesians 4:16). No one is called to be a spectator or to just pay the bills of those who do the work.

Ministry has more to do with how people touch others with the power of the gospel than with folding bulletins or refurbishing the church's kitchen or getting people to church so that the pastor can minister to them. All these types of activities can be classed "ministry," but ministry should not become so limited, trivialized, or superficialized. It will lack the potency to change the lives of those being touched. Transformation is what ministry is all about.

Teaching, counseling, discipling, and so on, duties often assigned to the pastor, are scripturally delegated to believers to do for one another. As one friend of mine said, "we cannot ignore it just because we don't like the cost."

Though a great idea, releasing people for significant ministry does not often translate into actuality. Vast numbers of people in our churches have tremendous ministry potential but find little or no outlet for that potential. Others are limited by church structures that prevent them from getting involved in meaningful ministry because they lack the professional credentialing. Some simply do not minister because they have never been appropriately trained while others suffer because of distrust by the very spiritual leadership called to release them.

If we are to see the present trend of American church decline reversed, we must release countless numbers of equipped believers to minister to existing needs. Every member of Christ's body has the potential to function in such a way if we are willing to reexamine our attitude, our actions, and address our objections. By using "EQUIP" as an acronym, I am attempting to address five oft-heard objections.

First - Efficiency. Most would agree that utilizing non-paid, non-staff people for ministry matters is not the most efficient means of operating an organization. A well oiled, in-the-same-building, paid staff or team of people is needed. The only problem is that it is not fully scriptural.

With different schedules, locations, demands, and priorities, church people present pastors with significant challenges. But this is life. Rocking a colicky baby at 2:00 a.m. hardly seems efficient, nor does measles, Little League schedules, school open-houses, and the such, which come a few years later. These only serve to reinforce the notion that life is not always efficient.

That is not to say that we abandon our attempts at improved efficiency, increased availability, and greater promptness but that we not use "efficiency" as a disqualification for involving the people. It will require work but the rewards are worth it. Ministry, like people, takes time.

Second - Qualified. It is true that those in professional ministry might possess superior training, experience, and resources. It is also true that mistakes will happen when people-led ministry begins to function.

However, it has been my experience that wisdom, insight, gifting, and spiritual maturity are not the sole domain of "the clergy." Millions of believers may not possess the theological-academic training the professionals do, but most of them are far more practical and understanding. They have no need to live in theological penthouses or function from theoretical "ivory towers." As far as mistakes go, history has proven that those classified "the ministers" have made their equal share, and in some cases, have disqualified themselves from the ministry by sinful behavior. This matter of competence includes far more than the development of the skills for ministry. Training of those who will be released is one key to effectively combating the "qualification" objection.

Third - Uniformed. When image, perfection, quality control, and uniformity are paramount, one makes the only conclusion possible; leave it to the professional. It is much easier to control ministry when we "do it" with only the professional staff. If we want a tidy operation then release of ministry to others will be of little interest (See Proverbs 14:4). Inconsistency should be expected -- in the motivations for ministry, the application of ministry, and the personal lives of those who minster. It is only after inviting people to share in authentic ministry that their weaknesses begin to show. Otherwise, such weaknesses remain hidden. It is easier not to give ministry responsibility in the first place but to leave it to the professional. Taking such an approach limits the development of the body of Christ and very well may suggest an unwillingness to invest the time necessary in developing consistent and systematic ways for people to "do" the ministry. "It's easier to do it myself" is the statement most often heard. Most know where that leads.

Fourth - Involved. "But pastor, you are more available to me than he is." Such an assumption tells the story. Just the opposite is true. The more we foster the notion that all ministry involvement must have the pastor's presence, the more we will bring destruction to the ministry, our personal lives, our families, our churches, etc. However, people need pastoral involvement in their lives. This particular situation appears to only be satisfied by building an increasingly larger professional staff but most have discovered by now that is not the answer. The answer lies with raising up a formidable team of people who are released to nurture, disciple, visit, pray, contact, pastorally care for . . . the people in Jesus' name. We must remember that equipping people for ministry is the scriptural means for taking care of the church and also the world. More, rather than less, of the people will receive ministry.

Fifth - Productive. "The proof is in the pudding," as we like to say. While many may object by suggesting a lack of effectiveness, the proof is that far more ministry takes place when there is the appropriate release of people into ministry. The professionals may resist because they feel threatened by releasing some of their "hands-on" work or because they will not receive the recognition. The people may consider themselves not as potentially productive, capable, or worthy to do "the work of the ministry." And the people of the church and community may object to common people doing ministry functions. They argue to wanting a real pastor, a real minister. However great the objections may be, greater results are the outgrowth of releasing people for the ministry. Simply put, because more are doing it more will be touched with Jesus' love. Seeing people love, encourage, and admonish each other proves there is fruit in multiplied ministry. Ministry benefits the recipient as well as the one performing it. The person involved in significant ministry becomes a more committed disciple of Jesus Christ.

3. Renew My Attitude for Leadership Selection and Development

Jesus' choice of the Twelve as his leadership team has been a surprise to many. With their frightening patterns of behavior and embarrassing traits they were not exactly prize recruits for a new spiritual organization. Despite their weaknesses, Jesus developed them into the foundational leaders of the first century church. Luke 9 reveals the risk Jesus took with them.

On their first official ministry assignment without Him, He gave them the actual power and authority (v. 1) necessary to fulfill their responsibility (vv. 2-6). Theirs was not just token busy work, but real, front line ministry responsibility. After completing their mission, they returned, gave account of their mission, then retreated with Jesus to the city of Bethsaida (v. 10). The remaining verses of the chapter reveal an astounding array of leadership failures. Notice:(11)

1. After seeing the miraculous hand of God work through them earlier (v. 6), they now lacked the faith necessary to feed the multitude assembled (vv. 11-13).
2. They fell asleep during a time of prayer when Jesus met with Moses and Elijah (vv. 28-32).
3. After awakening and seeing "the glory," Peter wanting to preserve the status quo, recommended the building of monuments to hold onto the experience (vv. 32-36).
4. Fear gripped the disciples. When Jesus healed the demonized boy (vv. 38-42), then spoke a statement that confused them, they were too intimidated by Him to ask the meaning of it (vv. 43-45).

5. They were highly competitive. They disputed with one another over who would be greatest and hold the most prestigious position while forgetting Jesus' message of serving others (vv. 46-48).

6. When they encountered a rival teacher, they tried to silence him by claiming absolute rights to Jesus' ministry (vv. 49-50).

7. They exhibited a vindictive and violent attitude for a group of individuals who were not hospitable toward Jesus. This attitude brought one of Jesus' strongest rebukes (vv. 51-56).

8. Boastfulness and overstatement were regrettable traits as well. Their unconditional promise to follow Jesus ended in failure a few years later at the cross (vv. 57-62).

Though the disciples were weak, lacking in faith, competitive, self-centered, unrealistic, and so on, Jesus kept working with them. In the end His hopes were realized. The book of Acts records the glorious story of the outcome of these men and others like them.

We can ill-afford to select on the basis of perfection. We must emulate Jesus' risk-taking, adventuresome way of choosing and developing leaders. Not many wise, or mighty, or noble were called. However, the foolish, the weak, the base and the despised were His specialty (I Corinthians 1:27-29). Let's reestablish a commitment to selecting and developing leaders who otherwise would normally be disqualified. Present and future generations are at stake.

The church is God's human agency for influencing the world and the needs of this world require that it operate according to its leader's instructions. Jesus Christ placed high importance upon discipleship, the ministry of every believer, and leadership development. The church must not forget why it is in the world.

One of America's most able and popular news commentators was reminiscing at the time of his retirement about one of his colleagues assigned to the nation's capital. He talked of the other commentator who, he said, "knew everyone worth knowing: the president, the diplomats, the senators, the president's cabinet, key bureaucrats, and the socially elite. He had the contacts; he was stuffed with information. There was only one problem," he said, "he never used it; He forgot what he was here for."(12) Jesus' church must not do the same.

The revitalization of existing churches and the birthing of new ones is key to the growth of the Kingdom of God in the United States and worldwide.

NOTES

1. Three sources contributed to these statistics:

    Aubrey Malphurs, **Vision America** (Grand Rapids, IL; Baker Books; 1994), pps. 9, 59.

    Patrick Johnstone, **Operation World** (Grand Rapids, IL; Zondervan Publishin House; 1993), pps. 563-567.

    Gary L. McIntosh, **Church Growth Network Newsletter** (San Bernardino, CA; 1993), p.1.

2. Comment was made by Leighton Ford.

3. Aubrey Malphurs, **Vision America**, p.128.

4. Paul Y. Cho, **Prayer: Key To Revival** (Waco, TX; Word Incoporated; 1984), p.10.

5. Will Durant, **The Story of Civilization - The Revormation** (NY, NY; Simon & Schuster, 1957), pps. 339-340.

6. **America's Great Revivals** (Minneapolis, MN; Dimension Books; 1968), pps. 12-20.

7. Ibid., pps. 73-94.

8. E.M. Bounds, **Power Through Prayer** (Chicago, IL; Moody Press), p.28.

9. These four statements, used widely, were regulary printed on our church bulletin's backside when I arrived at Living Word Christian Fellowship in 1993.

10. Jim Petersen, **Lifestyle Discipleship** (Colorado Springs, CO; NavPress; 1993), p.15.

11. An article titled, "Can Laity Do The Job?", was the inspiration for the comments. Published in **Metier, Dveloping Excellence in Faith and Work**, (Madision, WI; Marketplace Ministires; 1994), p.4.

12. Maxie D. Dunnam, **Mastering The New Testament**, Vol. 8; (Waco, TX; Word Incorporated; 1982), p. 203.